AN AMERICAN HISTORY:
OUR FOUNDATION
AND
MORAL COMPASS

WOODROW POLSTON

WOODROW POLSTON

AN AMERICAN HISTORY:

OUR FOUNDATION AND MORAL COMPASS

WOODROW POLSTON

AN AMERICAN HISTORY: OUR FOUNDATION AND MORAL COMPASS
Copyright © 2021 by Woodrow Polston. All rights reserved.

No part of this publication may be reproduced, stored in a retrieval system or transmitted in any way by any means, electronic, mechanical, photocopy, recording or otherwise without the prior permission of the author except as provided by USA copyright law.

This book is designed to provide accurate and authoritative information with regard to the subject matter covered. This information is given with the understanding that neither the author nor Polston House Publishing, LLC is engaged in rendering legal, professional advice.

The opinions expressed by the author are not necessarily those of Polston House Publishing, LLC.

Published by Polston House Publishing LLC
www.Polstonhouse.com

Book design copyright © 2016 by Polston House Publishing, LLC. All rights reserved.

Published in the United States of America

CONTENTS

Introduction		7
1	Founders of Freedom A Notable Few A New World Visions of the Future	11
2	Of Religious Virtue A Foundation of Faith Freedom Defined World Impact	23
3	Importance of Arms The 2nd Amendment Then and Now	33
4	Family Values Morals and Ethics A Standard of Integrity	41
5	Process of Restoration The Great Divide A Bridge Between	47
6	In Keeping Independence A Call for Global Government The Dangers of Big Tech Reformation or Ruin?	55

The Constitution	69
The Declaration of Independence	113
Select Writings and Documents	
"Give Me Liberty Or Give Me Death" by Patrick Henry	119
Boston Massacre Oration by Joseph Warren	125
Speech to the Virginia Convention by Patrick Henry	141
First Inaugural Address by George Washington	149
Farewell Address by George Washington	155
Notes	181
About the Author	185

INTRODUCTION

In the beginning, even before the land was known as the United States of America, Christians were among the first settlers to call it home. Considering that the nation was founded on the principles and integrity of the Judeo-Christian Bible, there is naturally a wealth of American Christian history to be contemplated.

Over the span of only a few centuries, the new world flourished immensely. And the church was no exception. Today, there are more than 300,000 church buildings in the United States. That would break down to an average of 12,000 per state.

According to a 2014 poll, about 70% of U.S. citizens profess attendance at a Christian church. In terms of missions, many countries around the world have received the Gospel of Jesus Christ as a result of our corporate church. Not only this, but the sick have been treated and healed. Countless people have been cared for, loved and many foreign churches have been planted by American missionaries and ministers.

This work in detail, reflects the record of America's Christian origin. As well as it's influence in politics, law, and every aspect of American life. It's past, present and future. The abstracts and certainty. The origin of our moral standards, the current provocation of culture and ultimate future onward. Also, the importance of upholding our Constitution.

What more can be said of such a great nation? What more desired of a free people? Can there be any doubt in all of creation that God has truly blessed such a land? I say, there can be no doubt at all!

Among the founding fathers, who would establish a free and brave new world, there was a collective knowledge of a Supreme Being, and the liberty that only He could provide. That liberty would serve as inspiration, and a foundation for our Constitution.

Today, the King James Bible, as well as the Constitution have been, by some, forgotten and discarded. Others have attacked, dismissed, and despised them.

The good news however, is that there remains yet many patriotic Americans, that hold them close to heart. Yes, even a vast number of Christian men and women, who still stand in agreement, that without these vital documents and writings, our freedom would not endure.

Let us recall the beginning, to consider the present. If need be that we change course, may we boldly move forward to forge the future.

I have included in this book, The United States Constitution, the Declaration of Independence, and other founding documents of interest. Of the which there cannot be too numerous in print for our benefit. Lest we forget!

"Of all the dispositions and habits which lead to political prosperity, religion and morality are indispensable supports. In vain would that man claim the tribute of patriotism, who should labor to subvert these great pillars of human happiness."
- George Washington[1]

1

Founders of Freedom

Of the many men that can be given ample credit, there are some that unquestionably stand out. One principle thing that remains true, is that the founding fathers were men of like mind, faith and determination. Had there been dramatic differences in their core beliefs, (as we see today in America) it is doubtful they would have achieved such an overwhelming success.

Today, it is the hope of many Americans, that our patriotic unity is rekindled. And many feel that it is a necessity, for our future as a prosperous nation.

Let us look now to some of the founders who would serve as prime examples of who we need to be today. Let us consider the former ways, as we work together to form the future and the destiny of our great nation!

A Notable Few

There can be little doubt, that anytime you hear the words 'Founding fathers' or 'Constitution', the first President of the United States comes to mind. And to consider the moral standing, faith and desires of the people, what could be more revealing than the character of the man they would elect to lead them.

George Washington
(February 22, 1732–December 14, 1799)

A military General, Statesman and political leader, George Washington served as the first President of the United States of America, from 1789 -1797. Presiding at the Constitutional convention of 1787, which established the United States Constitution and the Federal Government, He has been given the title of "Father of his country."

Let us consider who he was in terms of his faith and his beliefs. The following are a collection of some of his most notable quotes on the subject.

"It having pleased the Almighty Ruler of the universe to defend the cause of the United American States, and finally to raise up a powerful friend among the princes of the earth, to establish our

liberty and independence upon a lasting foundation, it becomes us to set apart a day for gratefully acknowledging the divine goodness, and celebrating the important event, which we owe to His divine interposition." -May 5th 1778 [1]

A letter to the thirteen Governors:

"I now make it my earnest prayer that God would have you, and the state over which you preside, in His holy protection...that He would most graciously be pleased to dispose us all to do justice, to love mercy, and to demean ourselves with that charity, humility, and pacific temper of mind, which were the characteristics of the divine Author of our blessed religion, and without an humble imitation of whose

example in these things, we can never hope to be a happy nation." - June 14th 1783 ²

"Almighty God; We make our earnest prayer that thou wilt keep the United States in thy Holy protection; and Thou wilt incline the hearts of the citizens to cultivate a spirit of subordination and obedience to Government; and entertain a brotherly affection and love for one another and for their fellow citizens of the United States at large, and particularly for their brethren who have served in the field.
And finally that thou wilt most graciously be pleased to dispose us all to do justice, to love mercy, and to demean ourselves with that charity, humility, and pacific temper of mind which were the characteristics of the divine Author of our blessed religion, and without a humble imitation of whose example in these things we can never hope to be a happy nation.
Grant our supplication, we beseech thee, through Jesus Christ our Lord. Amen." - Prayer for the United States of America. ³

The following statements made by President George Washington, are very telling concerning the founders thoughts on religious freedom.

"If I could have entertained the slightest apprehension that the Constitution framed by the Convention, where I had the honor to preside, might possibly endanger the religious rights of any ecclesiastical Society, certainly I would never have placed my signature to it;... I beg you will be persuaded that no one would be more zealous than myself to establish effectual barriers against... every species of religious persecution."
- *May 10th, 1789* [4]

"It shall still be my endeavor to manifest, by overt acts, the purity of my inclination for promoting the happiness of mankind, as well as the sincerity of my desires to contribute whatever may be in my power towards the preservation of the civil and religious liberties of the American people." - May 29th, 1789 [5]

    In recent times, a misguided interpretation of the 1st amendment of the Constitution has become more common. It emphasizes the importance of keeping religious values out of government. When in fact, the true purpose of the amendment would be to keep the government out of religion.

    It is clearly evident from the statements of Washington himself, that not only was he a Christian who helped form the government, but one who instilled his beliefs and values into it.

Let us consider others of the founders, and what more conclusions can be drawn by their statements of faith and conviction.

John Adams

(October 30th, 1735- July 4th, 1826)

The 2nd President of the United States, John Adams, was another example of great leadership and influence. Not only had he served as the Vice President under George Washington for eight years, he was a signer of the Declaration of Independence.

Notable accomplishments under his Presidency include the establishment of the Library of Congress, and the Department of the Navy. He too, like Washington, made bold declarations concerning his faith. As well as the importance of his faith based values for a free and peaceful society.

> *"Suppose a nation in some distant region should take the Bible for their only law book, and every member should regulate his conduct by the precepts there exhibited! Every member would be obliged in conscience, to temperance, frugality, and industry; to justice, kindness, and charity towards his fellow men; and to piety, love, and reverence toward Almighty God.... What a Eutopia, what a Paradise would this region be." - February 22nd, 1756* [6]

> *"Statesmen, my dear Sir, may plan and speculate for liberty, but it is Religion and Morality alone, which can establish the principles upon which freedom can securely stand. The only foundation of a free Constitution is pure virtue, and if this cannot be inspired into our people in a greater measure, than they have it now, they may change their Rulers and the forms of Government, but they will not obtain a lasting liberty." - June 21st, 1776* [7]

In this statement, Adams has made clear his opinion. It is Religion and Morality alone that must be our foundation, without which we will have no freedom. Without this Religion, Morality and virtue he said, the people could change their rulers and forms of Government. The consequences of doing such however would result in a loss of liberty.

Thomas Jefferson
(April 13, 1743 - July, 1826)

The third President of the United States of America. Thomas Jefferson was a prolific writer. He had much to say concerning the importance of our freedom.

"Almighty God, Who has given us this good land for our heritage; We humbly beseech Thee that we may always prove ourselves a people mindful of Thy favor and glad to do Thy will. Bless our land with honorable ministry, sound learning, and pure manners.
Save us from violence, discord, and confusion, from pride and arrogance, and from every evil way. Defend our liberties, and fashion into one united people the multitude brought hither out of many kindreds and tongues.

AN AMERICAN HISTORY: OUR FOUNDATION AND MORAL COMPASS

> *Endow with Thy spirit of wisdom those to whom in thy Name we entrust the authority of government, that there may be justice and peace at home, and that through obedience to Thy law, we may show forth Thy praise among the nations of the earth.*
> *In time of prosperity fill our hearts with thankfulness, and in the day of trouble, suffer not our trust in Thee to fail; all of which we ask through Jesus Christ our Lord, Amen."* [1]
> - March 4, 1805

These three men, served as the first three Presidents, whom the people of a free nation would look to for leadership. More than two hundred years later, little has changed. In that we still look to our President to lead us.

Today, America is made up of an ever increasingly diverse group of peoples, cultures and beliefs. This of course, warrants a new variety of political candidates. And considering that there are some dramatic differences in beliefs, our election of leaders becomes more important and pugnacious.

A New World

In the beginning, it was not so. The founding fathers aim was to form an immigration policy that would create unified Americans. That no matter the background, or country of origin, all people would blend together beneath the umbrella of our American beliefs.

Let us consider some of the thoughts and writings that the founding fathers shared on this subject.

> *"The name of American, which belongs to you in your national capacity, must always exalt the just pride of patriotism more than any appellation derived from local discriminations. With slight shades of difference, you have the same religion, manners, habits, and political principles."*- George Washington[7]

> *"The safety of a republic depends essentially on the energy of a common national sentiment; on a uniformity of principles and habits; on the exemption of the citizens from foreign bias and prejudice, and on the love of country which will almost invariably be found to be closely connected with birth, education, and family."* -Alexander Hamilton [6]

> *"When we are considering the advantages that may result from an easy mode of naturalization, we ought also to consider the cautions necessary to guard against abuses. It is no doubt very desirable that we should hold out as many inducements as possible for the worthy part of mankind to come and settle amongst us, and throw their fortunes into a common lot with ours. But why is this desirable? Not merely to swell the catalogue of people. No, sir, it is to increase the wealth and strength of the community; and those who acquire the rights of citizenship without adding to the strength or wealth of the community are not the people we are in want of ..."*
>
> *"What can be more reasonable than that when crowds of them [immigrants] come here, they should be forced to renounce everything contrary to the spirit of the Constitution?"* -James Madison [6]

Clearly, from such opinions, we see that the founders never envisioned a melting pot of diverse values and beliefs, at least not without conflict. No, they would hope for a new world where freedom and liberty would prevail. Made possible by a determined people of one mind, and one accord.

Many peoples have seen the light of this free world, shining as a beacon. And many have come to embrace it. But when did we fail to communicate to them the source of that light and freedom?

2

Of Religious Virtue

The most important, and fundamental, building block in the foundation of our country is fixed on our belief in God. How could we possibly explain the supernatural blessings this nation has been afforded, apart from there being a merciful, caring God who is watching over it?

Consider the nation of Israel for a moment, from whom our religious beliefs are derived. God himself, literally created the nation, according to the text in the book of Genesis.

> *"I will make you a great nation; I will bless you And make your name great; And you shall be a blessing. I will bless those who bless you, And I will curse him who curses you; And in you all the families of the earth shall be blessed."*
> Genesis 12:2-3

In recent years, there has been a growing effort to cloud the memory of our true history. In some, there seems to be a great desire to all but erase, and rewrite our history. There have even been prominent American figures that have stated that "America is not a Christian nation." And though there is indeed a liberal steering toward American secularism, we are still, and always have been a Christian nation.

A Foundation of Faith

To discover the truth of our origin, and the base of our beliefs, we need to look no further than our founding fathers. And there is no scarcity of books, documents, writings and lectures on the subject matter. Of the most notable documents, let us consider this excerpt;

In Congress, July 4, 1776

"When, in the course of human events, it becomes necessary for one people to dissolve the political bands which have connected them with another, and to assume among the powers of the earth, the separate and equal station to which the laws of nature and of nature's God entitle them, a decent respect to the opinions of mankind, requires that they should declare the causes which impel them to the separation. We hold these truths to be self-evident: that all men are created equal: that they are endowed by their Creator with certain unalienable rights: that among these are life, liberty, and the pursuit of happiness." [1]

- The Declaration of Independence

In this founding document, we find both the words 'God' and 'Creator'. Following is a short list of quotes from the signers of the Declaration of Independence. In their own words, let it be known who the instances of 'God' and 'Creator' are alluding to;

"In circumstances dark as these, it becomes us, as men and <u>Christians</u>, to reflect that, whilst every prudent measure should be taken to ward off the impending Judgements....All confidence must be withheld from the means we use; and reposed only on that God who rules in the Armies of Heaven, and without whose blessing the best human counsels are but foolishness.." -John Hancock [2]

"Religion is of general and public concern, and on it's support depend, in great measure, the peace and good order of government, the safety and happiness of the people. By our form of government, the

> *Christian religion is the established religion; and all sects and denominations of Christians are placed upon the same equal footing, and are equally entitled to protection in their religious liberty."-* Samuel Chase [3]

George Read, a signer of the Declaration of Independence, was also a U.S. Senator, and Chief Justice of the Supreme Court of Delaware. He also wrote the following requirements in the state of Delaware's Constitution:

> *"Every person who shall be chosen a member of either house, or appointed to any office or place of trust...shall... make and subscribe the following declaration, to wit: "I do profess faith in God the Father, and in Jesus Christ His only son, and in the Holy Ghost, one God, blessed for evermore; and I do acknowledge the holy scriptures of the Old and New Testament to be given by divine inspiration." -* George Read [4]

This requirement for those who would serve as Delaware's leaders, is a reflection of the standard set forth for rulers in the time of Moses. Consider the counsel given to Moses by his father-in-law Jethro;

> *"Hearken now unto my voice, I will give thee counsel, and God shall be with thee: be thou for the people to God-ward, that thou mayest bring the*

causes unto God: And thou shalt teach them ordinances and laws, and shalt shew them the way wherein they must walk, and the work that they must do. Moreover thou shalt provide out of all the people able men, such as fear God, men of truth, hating covetousness; and place such over them, to be rulers of thousands, and rulers of hundreds, rulers of fifties, and rulers of tens." Exodus 18: 19-21

"While we give praise to <u>God,</u> the supreme disposer of all events, for His interposition on our behalf, let us guard against the dangerous error of trusting in, or boasting of, an arm of flesh..." -John Witherspoon [5]

"The only foundation for a republic is to be laid in Religion. Without this there can be no virtue, and without virtue there can be no liberty, and liberty is the object and life of all republican governments." - Benjamin Rush [6]

"I have alternately been called an Aristocrat and a Democrat. I am neither. I am a <u>Christocrat</u>." - Benjamin Rush [7]

There can be little doubt, that those who signed the Declaration of Independence, were steeped in the practice of religion. Neither can we claim that their beliefs, were of any other origin than that of the Christian faith.

Our founders of this great nation, knew that without God and the Christian faith, there would be no basis for liberty, or enduring freedom.

Freedom Defined

I believe wholeheartedly, that America is the most exceptional nation on earth. It has welcomed all people without prejudice. And is referred to, after all, as 'the free world'. But would this nation offer such freedom without it's Christian foundation?

Consider the following statement, by American Revolutionary leader and five time Governor of the state of Virginia, Patrick Henry:

> *"It cannot be emphasized too strongly or too often that this great nation was founded, not by religionists, but by Christians; not on religions, but on the Gospel of Jesus Christ. For this very reason peoples of other faiths have been afforded asylum, prosperity, and freedom of worship here." - Patrick Henry* [8]

With this statement from Patrick Henry, we may conclude, or at the very least strongly suggest, that Christianity is not exclusively beneficial to Christians.

The Christian faith and way of life, has indeed opened wide the doors of security, and prosperity for all peoples.

But what basis does freedom have in the Christian faith one might ask? Referring to the Bible, we find a wealth of support:

"For you, brethren, have been called to liberty; only do not use liberty as an opportunity for the flesh, but through love serve one another." - Galatians 5:13

"Now the Lord is the Spirit; and where the Spirit of the Lord is, there is liberty." -2 Corinthians 3:17

"And you shall know the truth, and the truth shall make you free." -John 8:32

"because the creation itself also will be delivered from the bondage of corruption into the glorious liberty of the children of God." - Romans 8:21

"Therefore if the Son makes you free, you shall be free indeed." -John 8:36

And so with the foundation of freedom, all peoples of different beliefs, have been afforded citizenship in the land of liberty. Even despite the fact that many resent, and even hate the true origin of our foundation.

Have we forgotten that our founders warned us, that without our principles in faith, our freedom would not endure? Have we perhaps bought into the lie, that says our religious values have no place in our politics?

Far too long have we entertained the notion, that there is a fortified wall between the two. This was not the intent of the founding fathers. It was not the opinion of Politicians, or Preachers. Both on the sides of religion and politics, were in agreement on the matter. Consider the following statement from a great early American Author and Preacher:

> *"The church must take right ground in regards to politics… The time has come for Christians to vote for honest men, and take consistent ground in politics or the Lord will curse them…*
> *God cannot sustain this free and blessed country, which we love and pray for, unless the Church will take right ground. Politics are a part of a religion in such a country as this, and Christians must do their duty to their country as a part of their duty to God…God will bless or curse this nation according to the course Christians take in politics."* -Charles Finney [9]

World Impact

Just as the Christian faith has been beneficial to Immigrants that do not identify as Christians, so too has it been a blessing around the globe. It was early on that missions work started in America to spread the Word of God across the entire world. On February 19, 1812, Adoniram Judson left for India as one of the first American missionaries.

One year later, he found himself in Burma and devoted his life to bringing the gospel to the Burmese people. It took him six years to see his first convert, and he buried three wives on the mission field, all to plant seeds for a great harvest in Burma.[10]

Adoniram Judson

Since that very first mission from the nation of America, countless people around the world have not only received the Word of God, but have also been fed, clothed, cared for, and treated with medicines.

As a young nation and ultimately a new world, America helped foreign countries come to God through its missions work, and immigrants from many countries became Christians through its way of life.

It is then very safe, and factual to say, that the whole world has reaped the benefits of America having been rooted in Christianity. And God willing, it will continue to be true well into the future.

WOODROW POLSTON

3

Importance of Arms

Our founding fathers understood the necessity for an armed population. And that the consequences of disarmament would result in our ruin. For without the ability to stand our ground, with proper defense, there could be no hope for enduring freedom.

By expressing the weight of well armed citizens, they were not only concerned about defense against a foreign enemy, but also for a means of a blockade to tyranny from within.

The 2nd Amendment

> "A well regulated Militia, being necessary to the security of a free State, the right of the people to keep and bear Arms, shall not be infringed." [11]

Our Constitution is complete with 27 amendments. And I believe that the 2nd amendment, made up of 27 words, is the catalyst to the cement that holds them all together.

Above all else I believe this; that if the 2nd amendment were to be diluted or dissolved, every other amendment that protects our rights as free citizens, would quickly disappear as well. And according to the following quotes, the founding fathers strongly believed the same:

> "And what country can preserve its liberties, if its rulers are not warned from time to time, that this people preserve the spirit of resistance? Let them take arms...The tree of liberty must be refreshed from time to time, with the blood of patriots and tyrants." - Thomas Jefferson [1]

> "A militia, when properly formed, are in fact the people themselves...and include all men capable of bearing arms." - Richard Henry Lee [2]

> "The great object is, that every man be armed.... Every one who is able may have a gun." -Patrick Henry [3]

> "Little more can reasonably be aimed at with respect to the people at large than to have them properly armed and equipped." -Alexander Hamilton [4]

> "...arms like laws discourage and keep the invader and plunderer in awe...Horrid mischief would ensue were the good deprived of the use of them." -Thomas Payne [5]

"Those who would give up essential Liberty to purchase a little temporary Safety, deserve neither Liberty nor Safety." Benjamin Franklin [6]

"Before a standing army can rule, the people must be disarmed; as they are in almost every kingdom in Europe. The supreme power in America cannot enforce unjust laws by the sword; because the whole body of the people are armed...." - Noah Webster [7]

Then and Now

During the frontier days of the seventeen hundreds, the most advanced weapon in hand, was the musket. A long-barreled gun that required the use of messy gun powder, and the loading of a ball to be fired.

To witness the reloading process, it would seem as though one were conducting a frantic science experiment, every time they prepared to fire a shot. The rate of fire, at best was 3-6 rounds per minute, with a muzzle velocity of 1,300- 1,800 feet per second. [8]

Today, the United States Military uses the M16 rifle, and the M249 light machine gun. Which use the NATO 5.56 mm. with a cyclic rate of fire of 700-950 rounds per minute, with a muzzle velocity of 3,000-3,150 feet per second. [9]

While these two weapons are beyond impressive, there are many other guns, weapons, machinery, and not to mention explosives that are found in the government's arsenal.

Politicians that are seemingly caught up in endless pursuit of gun control, would like for American citizens to be ignorant of the fact that our 2nd amendment rights have already been infringed. In that while the government's weapons technology has advanced dramatically, citizens are not allowed to purchase automatic weapons. Thus, leaving them with the much slower, single shot rate of fire per trigger pull. Their argument is simply this;

> 'You don't need automatic weapons for hunting. You don't need high capacity magazines for deer!'

And in this only, are they correct. As a hunter and sportsman no one knows this better than myself. When I am deer hunting during rifle season, I often load only two or three shells into my 30.06 rifle. When that magical moment happens, that my deer has presented a clear and ethical shot, I fire one round that is chambered, to seal the deal.

But the 2nd amendment is not about hunting. Neither is it about sport shooting. No, we have the 2nd amendment for the purpose that it states; to maintain *"The security of a free state."*

If it were up to many of these Politicians today, we would only be allowed to have single shot muskets at best. Though they would certainly prefer us to be completely unarmed.

More and more, we are hearing calls for a ban on the popular military style AR15 and AK47 rifles. Both are semi-automatic weapons, that accept 30 and 40 round magazines. Imagine if we were only allowed to own handguns, shotguns, and rifles that do not accept high capacity magazines. The odds would clearly be in the enemy's favor, in the event of an armed conflict, wouldn't they?

Clearly, the Politicians who desire to keep their power and position, want nothing more than to remove any possibility of overthrow and removal, in the event that they have become tyrannical.

However, it is seemingly impossible already. For even if the powers that be were to become tyrannical, they would simply label American Patriots as domestic terrorists, and have them killed or imprisoned.

Honestly, for many reasons, one could say that there is tyranny already. One example, is in the fact that the Government, and their security can possess and use automatic weapons. But as to us the citizens, it is forbidden.

"Tyranny is defined as that which is legal for the government but illegal for the citizenry." - **Thomas Jefferson** [10]

Also, there is a common argument made by those who seek gun control, that being a Christian and owning such guns is somehow an oxymoron. While it is true, that Christianity is a religion of peace, we must acknowledge that those who are peacemakers are seldom unarmed.

I would offer for example, the following instance of Jesus Himself instructing His disciples to arm themselves;

"Then He said to them, "But now, he who has a money bag, let him take it, and likewise a knapsack; and he who has no sword, let him sell his garment and buy one." Luke 22:36

Consider this, for the sake of peace and safety. Those who advocate to ban our guns and reduce our 2nd amendment rights, are actually, and extremely, pro-violence. Because they are attempting to instigate what would possibly be, the bloodiest civil war in our history. Knowing well that patriotic Americans would never surrender the very rights and liberties, that our ancestors through much sacrifice, made possible.

If not for fear of being labeled a right wing conspiracy theorist, one might question the motives of those who seek to defund law enforcement, while pitting them against armed citizens who refuse to surrender their firearms. Does it not seem as though it would be a dream realized for those who hate both law enforcement and law abiding armed citizens?

If it were truly out of concern for innocent victims of gun violence, that drives the gun control advocates, where is their concern for the innocent blood of the millions of aborted babies that die in the womb? Is there only enough compassion in the world for certain types of innocent victims? Are there any kind of victims in the world more innocent and helpless than these children?

Sadly, our society is treading in a dangerous direction. Giving no heed to the hazard signs. Giving no place for correction. Refusing to be humbled.

We are fast approaching a dismal state, where we have war in the name of peace. Intolerance in the name of tolerance. Hate in the name of love. Injustice in the name of justice. And ultimately, evil in the name of good. It is paramount for our posterity, that we turn again to our former ways of wisdom, kindness, charity, patriotism and compassion for our fellow Americans.

The fact is simply this, that our Constitution is clear, in that we have the right to defend ourselves. And that right, as the founding fathers stated;

"Shall not be infringed." [11]

4

Family Values

Hard work and determination are the make up of American history. Hand in hand go the ethics and values of the American family. We honor God and country. We support our family and we defend our land. And with whatever remains after this, we help and support those who are less fortunate.

Morals and Ethics

From the time that the war was officially waged on family values, and more specifically on Christian family values, the results have been catastrophic. When prayer was removed from public schools in 1962, the biggest concerns regarding students were dress code violation, chewing gum in class, and running in the halls. Today, the concerns are murder, drug addiction, rape, alcohol abuse, and teen pregnancy.

As a result of numerous deadly shooting incidents that have occurred in public schools, many citizens have sought a solution to prevent these senseless acts. Some feel that tighter gun control will be the answer, and communist regimes such as China have even stated that American citizens should indeed be disarmed. Is that not a sign that we should keep our arms or what?

Creating an unstable environment at school was not enough, so the home life of average American citizens was also a key target. As the need for more income became evident in the early nineteen sixties, both parents found themselves working full time jobs.

As a result, children without a permanent homebody would depend more on the government-run schools (Where God was being removed). Additionally, some children would learn their moral values from television. Through the outlets of the media, which include television, film, commercials, music, and magazines, a campaign of brainwashing that has seemingly destroyed the moral values of our society.

In popular women's magazines, There is no mention of family or children. Alternative lifestyle options are pushed through these outlets and basically, everything that contradicts the way that we should live according to the word of God.

Let us consider two fundamental instructions that God gave to man in the beginning:

"Therefore a man shall leave his father and mother and be joined to his wife, and they shall become one flesh." - Genesis 2:24

"Then God blessed them, and God said to them, "Be fruitful and multiply." - Genesis 1:28

And this was actually the first commandment that God gave to mankind, to be fruitful and multiply! Clearly, the motives behind abortion, and unfruitful alternatives are to disobey the commandment, and to disregard our purpose. God has given us the miracle of procreation, to fill the earth with mankind.

A Standard of Integrity

Above all else, we must have restoration in our integrity. The word *integrity would be defined in a dictionary as this:*

"The quality of being honest and having strong moral principles, moral uprightness."

There seems to be a growing hatred for the truth. Americans have become all too eager for comforting lies, in a pursuit to avoid the truth at all cost. But we cannot keep the truth shut up. We cannot keep it hidden. Jesus said this:

"And you shall know the truth, and the truth shall make you free." - John 8:32

"No one lights a lamp and then puts it under a basket. Instead, a lamp is placed on a stand, where it gives light to everyone in the house." - Matthew 5:15

Its been said that a man is only as good as his word. And there can be little dignity without there first being integrity. And so likewise, a nation, is only as good as it's integrity.

"I am sure that in estimating every man's value either in private or public life, a pure integrity is the quality we take first into calculation, and that learning and talents are only the second." - Thomas Jefferson [1]

With the rise of political correctness, and the demand that the general populous accept and agree with everything that others believe, we are approaching dangerous points of no return. How did this happen? Have we become so soft, so sheltered that this was unavoidable? Is it time that we toughen up? That we take on hardships and shun the easy paths?

Consider the brutal determination of the founders for a moment. In the freezing Winter of 1777, General George Washington was facing the burden of a lack of supplies for his troops, who were camped at Valley Forge. The soldiers were dying at a rate of 12 per day. They were without blankets, and didn't even have shoes for their feet. George Washington recorded the following:

"No history now extant can furnish an instance of an army's suffering such uncommon hardships as ours has done and bearing them with the same patience and fortitude. To see men without clothes to cover their nakedness, without blankets to lie on, without shoes (for the want of which their marches might be traced by the blood from their feet)…and submitting without a murmur, is a proof of patience and obedience which in my opinion can scarce be paralleled." [2]

Do Americans still have this determination? Shall our Grandchildren be amazed and inspired, or shall they be astonished and ashamed?

WOODROW POLSTON

5

Process of Restoration

One thing that can surely be agreed upon, if nothing else at all, is that without a renewed sense of unity, our fate as a nation is doomed. And while such a fate would be most desirable of our enemies, it should be the ultimate dread of our citizens. But the question which demands an answer here is simply this; how will we, as a nation, so divided, come together in such unity?

Without going off into deep study and theory, the best answer is simply this: It will take an act of God. And after all, this is actually the most biblical answer, and solution to a national emergency. Consider the following text from the book of 2nd Chronicles:

> *"If my people, which are called by my name, shall humble themselves, and pray, and seek my face, and turn from their wicked ways; then will I hear from heaven, and will forgive their sin, and will heal their land."* 2 Chronicles 7:14

The text reveals four actions that we must do to bring about restoration. To humble ourselves, to pray, to seek his face, and turn from our wickedness.

The Great Divide

Although the Republican and Democratic parties have been around since the early nineteenth century, they have never been more combative than present day.

Among our first leaders, it was never desired that there be such a division. In fact, our first President, George Washington warned against the dangers of factions in his farewell address;

> *"All obstructions to the execution of the laws, all combinations and associations, under whatever plausible character, with the real design to direct, control, counteract, or awe the regular deliberation*

and action of the constituted authorities, are destructive of this fundamental principle, and of fatal tendency. They serve to organize faction, to give it an artificial and extraordinary force; to put, in the place of the delegated will of the nation the will of a party, often a small but artful and enterprising minority of the community; and, according to the alternate triumphs of different parties, to make the public administration the mirror of the ill-concerted and incongruous projects of faction, rather than the organ of consistent and wholesome plans digested by common counsels and modified by mutual interests.

However combinations or associations of the above description may now and then answer popular ends, they are likely, in the course of time and things, to become potent engines, by which cunning, ambitious, and unprincipled men will be enabled to subvert the power of the people and to usurp for themselves the reins of government, destroying afterwards the very engines which have lifted them to unjust dominion."-George Washington [8]

Political parties can be in such opposition to each other, that they lose sight of what is right and true, in pursuit of victory for their party. The purposes of our Congress are perverted and unfulfilled, when the parties war against one another. Rather than working for the people.

In the Fall of 2019, on Columbus day, I announced that I would be running a campaign for State Representative. Though we had just bought a house and moved to this district two months prior,(and were relatively unknown in the area) I gave it a shot.

My brother in law had been one of several people to encourage me. He also, was running for Congress in Texas' 31st district, as an Independent candidate.

Though I shared his sentiment of 'People not Parties', I was on the Republican ticket. I was well aware of how hard it can be to win a race as an Independent.

The area we had moved to had seen a significant shift in previous years, from Democrat to Republican. In fact, the State of Missouri had more than 180 Republican candidates file for the house in 2020. And there were approximately 50 districts that had no Democrat candidates at all!

What it all came down to, for me, when identifying as a Republican, were three big issues:

1. *Religious liberty*

I was aware of a left wing agenda, that would encroach upon the freedom of the church. There seemed to be a left leaning tendency, to force ones beliefs onto others. Such instances for example, include the desire to hold legally accountable, those who would refuse to offer services that are conflicting with their religious convictions.

The interest of seeing the church lose it's tax exempt status. Which is a discussion worthy of a book all it's own. Seriously, think about it for a moment. Consider all the church funds and programs that feed, cloth and support the needy in your area. Church benevolent funds pay for utilities. Electric, gas and water bills are commonly taken care of for people in need of assistance.

Imagine, not only in your area, but across the entire nation, what would happen if the church was forced to pay the government taxes! Would those left wing politicians pick up the tab for those in need? Of course not.

2. *The 2nd Amendment*

It's no secret that the left tend to be anti-gun rights. And we know where the founding fathers stood on the importance of this subject. Without the means to defend ourselves, with the use of adequate arms, we would be witness to the death of freedom as we know it.

3. *Abortion*

Make no mistake, the single most important moral issue that we face today, is abortion. The legality of which was brought about in 1973, by plaintiff Norma McCorvey, also known as Jane Roe (Roe vs. Wade.)

This legal procedure, will surely go down in history, as a great American atrocity. It has terminated more than 50 million unborn children. And it is very telling, that even Norma McCorvey herself, denounced it, and spent the latter part of her life in protest of it.

As I see it, these are the three most important issues that have divided the parties. And on such principle matters, how can there be an agreement? Is it even a possibility? Let us consider the steps that we can each take, to work toward a goal of common good and unity.

A Bridge Between

As the scripture in the beginning of the chapter stated, we must humble ourselves. To have unity, there must be humility. There is such a hostile political environment today, that one would rather curse and slander the opposition, than to pray for them! It takes a certain level of humility to pray for someone that is in opposition to you.

Though it may be quite difficult at times to do, we know that we should put others before ourselves. And we should respect others, even above ourselves. Achieving this, requires the casting aside of our differences, long enough to acknowledge that every person deserves to be heard and respected.

As Christians, we know that every human life is created in the image of God. Therefore, we should look upon our fellow man as a direct reflection of God. When we do this, a higher demand of respect will become evident.

While brotherly love, unity and perfect harmony will not exist without tolerance and acceptance, neither will it be so in demanding that others be forced to accept that which they do not agree with. It can become a dangerous new territory if we are forced to agree with that which others believe. If a man believes he is a woman, now he can enter into the women's restroom. If a man identifies as a child, can he now bring a lawsuit against his employer for breaking child labor laws? Or shall an adult be dismissed of pedophilia if they identify as a child? Scary stuff we are facing, isn't it?

We must return to common sense. And yes, there is plenty of it remaining. But we have to wake up and speak the truth, in love.

WOODROW POLSTON

6

In Keeping Independence

"If we lose freedom here, there is no place to escape to. This is the last stand on earth." - Ronald Reagan[11]

As much as we love our freedom and independence, there are some among us who despise it. Our liberty was given us at no small cost. But by the blood, sweat and tears of Patriots. Our resolve must be as theirs. We must keep our freedom. The liberties that we let slip today, our children will fight and die for tomorrow.

Among the greatest dangers to our independence, is the shift toward globalism. This, of course, has been many years in the making. Let us consider the issue, and it's implications.

A Call For Global Government

The establishment of the United Nations was a significant step toward global government. Having come into existence on October 24, 1945, the United Nations headquarters is located in New York City and was initiated by American president Franklin D. Roosevelt.

The creation of the UN was an attempt to succeed in the prevention of war and disarmament, where the league of nations, which was initiated by American president Woodrow Wilson, had failed.

Today, there are 193 member states that have been swallowed up by the organization. Here at home, the UN has control of all American landmarks, such as the Statue of Liberty, Independence hall, Monticello, Yellowstone, the Grand Canyon, the Great Smoky Mountains, and on and on.

What is more disturbing than the amount of American land that is under UN control is what they could soon potentially do with our money. In the second term for President Obama, which began in 2012, it was expected that the UN would tap into the pockets of Americans for tobacco taxes, carbon taxes, and numerous other taxes that will be redistributed around the globe.

Along with the ridiculous taxes, we also had the United Nations Arms Trade Treaty to contend with. Negotiated at a global conference in New York City in July of 2012, it would allow the UN to regulate the international trade of conventional weapons. Of the 193 member states, there were only 24 countries that abstained from the treaty.

Increasingly, the attempts to disarm the American people are evident. If you have studied biblical prophecy, you know that the end result of man's rule on the earth is a one world government system.

With the prophetic time clock ticking at a quickening pace, it only becomes more evident that we are growing dangerously closer to serious changes. And when world leaders are openly discussing a new world order, we should certainly take them serious.

Below is a list of quotes from around the world that reveal to us that something is definitely in the works behind the scenes.

> *"His task will be to develop an overall strategy for America in this period when, really, a new world order can be created. It's a great opportunity, it isn't just a crisis." (Henry Kissinger speaking of Obama, CNBC interview)* [2]

> *"All nations must come together to build a stronger global regime." (Barack Obama on new world order, presidential speech)* [3]

> *"Climate bill will help bring about global governance...but it is the awareness itself that will drive the change and one of the ways it will drive the change is through global governance and global agreements." (Al Gore on new world order, speech on climate change)* [4]

We need a global new deal...a grand bargain between the countries and continents of this world. (UK Prime Minister Gordon Brown, speech before G20 summit) [5]

Not only do we have evidence that there are secret plans being laid out regarding the future one world order, but we see that they have been in the works for quite some time. Let us consider what former presidents and US leaders have said concerning a secret agenda, dating as far back as more than a century ago.

"Some of the biggest men in the United States, in the field of commerce and manufacture, are afraid of something. They know that there is a power somewhere so organized, so subtle, so watchful, so interlocked, so complete, so pervasive, that they had better not speak above their breath when they speak in condemnation of it." (Woodrow Wilson) [6]

"For we are opposed, around the world, by a monolithic and ruthless conspiracy, that relies primarily on covert means for expanding it's sphere of influence, on infiltration instead of invasion, on subversion instead of elections, on intimidation instead of free choice, on guerrillas by night, instead of armies by day, it is a system which has conscripted, vast material and human resources into the building of a tightly knit, highly efficient

machine that combines military, diplomatic, intelligence, economic, scientific, and political operations. It's preparations are concealed, not published. It's mistakes are buried, not headlined. It's dissenters silenced, not praised." (JFK speech) [7]

"All of us will ultimately be judged on the effort we have contributed to building a New World Order." (Robert Kennedy) [8]

If these quotes from world leaders are not enough to sell you on the fact that there is a new world order in the works, maybe you need it written in stone. In that case, for the sake of proving this, it is in fact literally written in stone, right here at home in the United States of America.

Known as the American Stonehenge, or more commonly referred to as the Georgia Guidestones [9], in Elbert County, Georgia, stands the mysterious granite monument with apocalyptic references. Erected in 1979, an unknown person under the pseudonym RC Christian hired Elberton Granite Finishing Company to build the large structure. Standing nearly twenty feet tall, a total of six granite slabs weighing 237,746 pounds, stand astronomically aligned.

The astronomical features include a channel through the stone indicating the celestial pole. A horizontal slot indicates travel of the sun. And sunbeam through the capstone marks noontime throughout the year. On the edges of the square have names of four ancient languages written on them—Babylonian, Classical Greek, Sanskrit, and Ancient Egyptian. And in modern language, there are eight listed, including English, Spanish, Swahili, Hindi, Hebrew, Arabic, Chinese, and Russian. A separate tablet in the ground reads the following: "Let these be guide stones to an age of reason." And on the guide stones themselves, the following ten guidelines for humanity are written:

1. Maintain humanity under 500,000,000 in perpetual balance with nature.
2. Guide reproduction wisely- improving fitness and diversity.
3. Unite humanity with a living new language.
4. Rule passion-faith-tradition and all things with tempered reason.
5. Protect people and nations with fair laws and just courts.
6. Let all nations rule internally resolving external disputes in a world court.
7. Avoid petty laws and useless officials.
8. Balance personal rights with social duties.
9. Prize truth-beauty-love seeking harmony with the infinite.
10. Be not a cancer on the earth-leave room for nature-leave room for nature.

While some have hailed the stones as a call to rational thinking, others have dubbed them the ten commandments of the Antichrist! There are many theories as to who is responsible for their existence, which include a long list of secret societies that are considered to be connected to the elite world group known as the Illuminati.

However, there has been no further knowledge gained in the thirty-two years that they have been standing.

No one has come forward to take credit for the work, and no one has been found to offer an explanation. While the entire exhibit screams new world order, the most disturbing inscription is the call for maintaining humanity under five hundred million. Considering that there are more than 7 billion people on the earth today, this would seem to be a call for the extermination of more than 6.5 billion people.

As we know according to scripture, there will be wars in the last days that decimate the earth's population, and it is likely that these wars will be orchestrated by the world's elite. Who have the mind-set of these guidelines that are written in stone.

The Dangers of Big Tech

One of the most shocking things that I have witnessed in my adult life, happened in 2021, when social media giants silenced and shut down the President of the United States! As the big tech companies continue to swell in power, the possibilities of herding the masses becomes more real. And to think, that all of this was made possible by computers and microchips!

The invention of the microchip is credited to Jack Kilby, who was born in 1923 in Jefferson City, Missouri.[10] He created the first integrated circuit while working for Texas Instruments in 1958. Since that time, microchips have become an essential part of our daily life. When the word *microchip* comes up, most of us think of computers, cell phones, game systems, etc. However, it goes much deeper than that.

Microchips have now found a home in everything from football helmets to toilets. And depending on where you shop for clothing, you could even be wearing a microchip yourself, with certain retailers including a microchip the size of a grain of sand in the tags of clothing items.

With computerized restrooms, Aqua One Technologies has presented a toilet[11] that has an automatic shutoff in the event of a leak. And Japanese company Toto has a smart toilet that reads health-related data from the user's urine and sends the information to the user's physician.

Another odd use of modern microchips has been presented by a company in Pennsylvania and is called the memory medallion.[12] It is a coin-sized steel-encased microchip for tombstones. It tells the story of the deceased in photos, audio, and video. It can be activated when a visitor points their Internet-enabled cell phone at it.

The microchips that are raising eyebrows and creating conspiracy theories however are the likes of those created by such companies as Applied Digital Solutions and Alien Technologies. Applied Digital Solutions is the company that created the highly controversial verichip,[13] also known as the Digital Angel. With the use of GPS/satellite communications, the Verichip[4] can be implanted in both animals and humans for tracking and location purposes.

While millions of pets have been implanted with the RFID (radio frequency identification) chips, there are now a growing number of people who are receiving these implants as well. With the FDA-approved microchips, there are many possibilities being promoted, such as mandating the implants for all US soldiers and eventually all US citizens through the new health care system.

It is proposed that all health care recipients will be required to pay a monthly fee for the use of their implants. All the patient's health records will be contained within the chip and can be reviewed by medical staff by simply using a RFID scanner.

Eventually, it is highly likely that all human beings will be required to fuse this technology into their person.

With all the advantages that are being presented, such as medical and financial uses, we could easily see the evolution of a chipped society quickly come to pass. If a new monetary system is established and a one-world currency presented, it will likely involve the use of a card or microchip and be completely digital.

When the new monetary system is established, multitudes of people will be forced to accept an implant in order to maintain a banking account. As we know, no one will be able to buy or sell lest they have the mark of the beast. We are witnessing the worldwide collapse of the current monetary system. By the time the world powers have completed the economic crisis that they have created, society will be willing to accept any solution that they have to offer.

What many people do not realize is that they can already be tracked and easily located with the use of microchips and the thousands of satellites that are in orbit. Really, the only difference between having a microchip implant is that you will be aware that you are being monitored and tracked. Right now you can be tracked by your cell phone, and your conversations can be recorded even when your not on the phone.

Your vehicle can be tracked and located with GPS, clothing with RFID chips, etc. It is unbelievable to watch society willingly step into such an obvious snare, and what is the advantage?

You have a portable phone. You don't get lost or ask for directions with your vehicle's GPS. How did our ancestors survive? What would they think of our modern technology? They would probably view us as helpless simpletons who have to depend on technology to even use a toilet!

We must do all that we can to uphold our independence. We cannot exchange our freedom for political correctness. Nor can we give in to tyranny for false peace and security. Many are familiar with the saying 'What would Jesus do?' And that is a great question. To add to it, I would ask you this, what would our Founding Fathers do?

Reformation or Ruin?

I believe many would agree, that we are facing a point of no return status in our country. The problem with our agreement on this however is complex. For we are divided by opinions. Half of us claim to have the solution, while the other half claim that the very solution is in fact the problem. Where can you go from there?

The biggest question may perhaps no longer be 'What is the point of no return?' but rather 'What is on the other side of no return? Civil war? Endless unrest? A new form of government? Utter and hopeless ruin?

What is most unfortunate, and yet undeniably true, is that there is a portion of the population who would love to see the ruin of the United States. We know this not only to be true abroad, having enemy states around the world, but also here at home.

But being in such opposition one to another, how do we know which group is desirous of our ruin? The answer is quite simple really. The group of people who seek to abandon our Constitution. Discredit our founders, and despise our religion. Those who seek a new way that is contrary to our fundamental principles.

Now most of us would agree that our country is not perfect. One thing that is crystal clear to me, is the desperate and immediate need for tax reform. We pay too many taxes, which are wasted by politicians with too little accountability. As Americans, we do not want our tax dollars being handed over to foreign nations for frivolous endeavors. Especially those nations that aren't even allies

Our only hope for restoration, is to kindle the desire for American revival. A revival of our economy. A revival of our creed. A revival of our purpose and dreams. A revival of inspiration and good intentions. We must each look into the mirror and ask, 'What can I do to spark this revival?'.

As for me, there are some very simple ways that I am attempting to do this. It starts at home, with each one of us. I work hard to provide for my family. I do my best to serve faithfully in my church, neighborhood and community. As challenging as it may be at times, I do my best to stay positive.

The principle thing however, is that I am doing my best to be led of God. For there are many among us that seek to do good of their own accord, without the direction and consideration of God. Jesus said this *"There is none good but God."* How then do we have so many people that claim to be doing good works apart from the counsel and direction of God?

I hope that we see restoration in this land. I know that many of us are praying to God for such an outcome. And as the Word says *"With God, all things are possible."* Therefore let us believe it will be so. Amen.

WOODROW POLSTON

The United States Constitution

*"**We the People** of the United States, in Order to form a more perfect Union, establish Justice, insure domestic Tranquility, provide for the common defence, promote the general Welfare, and secure the Blessings of Liberty to ourselves and our Posterity, do ordain and establish this Constitution for the United States of America."*

Article. I.

Section. 1.

All legislative Powers herein granted shall be vested in a Congress of the United States, which shall consist of a Senate and House of Representatives.

Section. 2.

The House of Representatives shall be composed of Members chosen every second Year by the People of the several States, and the Electors in each State shall have the Qualifications requisite for Electors of the most numerous Branch of the State Legislature.
No Person shall be a Representative who shall not have attained to the Age of twenty five Years, and been seven Years a Citizen of the United States, and who shall not, when elected, be an Inhabitant of that State in which he shall be chosen.

Representatives and direct Taxes shall be apportioned among the several States which may be included within this Union, according to their respective Numbers, which shall be determined by adding to the whole Number of free Persons, including those bound to Service for a Term of Years, and excluding Indians not taxed, three fifths of all other Persons. The actual Enumeration shall be made within three Years after the first Meeting of the Congress of the United States, and within every subsequent Term of ten Years, in such Manner as they shall by Law direct. The Number of Representatives shall not exceed one for every thirty Thousand, but each State shall have at Least one Representative; and until such enumeration shall be made, the State of New Hampshire shall be entitled to chuse three, Massachusetts eight, Rhode-Island and Providence Plantations one, Connecticut five, New-York six, New Jersey four, Pennsylvania eight, Delaware one, Maryland six, Virginia ten, North Carolina five, South Carolina five, and Georgia three.

When vacancies happen in the Representation from any State, the Executive Authority thereof shall issue Writs of Election to fill such Vacancies.

The House of Representatives shall chuse their Speaker and other Officers; and shall have the sole Power of Impeachment.

Section. 3.

The Senate of the United States shall be composed of two Senators from each State, chosen by the Legislature thereof, for six Years; and each Senator shall have one Vote.
Immediately after they shall be assembled in Consequence of the first Election, they shall be divided as equally as may be into three Classes. The Seats of the Senators of the first Class shall be vacated at the Expiration of the second Year, of the second Class at the Expiration of the fourth Year, and of the third Class at the Expiration of the sixth Year, so that one third may be chosen every second Year; and if Vacancies happen by Resignation, or otherwise, during the Recess of the Legislature of any State, the Executive thereof may make temporary Appointments until the next Meeting of the Legislature, which shall then fill such Vacancies.
No Person shall be a Senator who shall not have attained to the Age of thirty Years, and been nine Years a Citizen of the United States, and who shall not, when elected, be an Inhabitant of that State for which he shall be chosen.
The Vice President of the United States shall be President of the Senate, but shall have no Vote, unless they be equally divided.
The Senate shall chuse their other Officers, and also a President pro tempore, in the Absence of the Vice

President, or when he shall exercise the Office of President of the United States.

The Senate shall have the sole Power to try all Impeachments. When sitting for that Purpose, they shall be on Oath or Affirmation. When the President of the United States is tried, the Chief Justice shall preside: And no Person shall be convicted without the Concurrence of two thirds of the Members present.

Judgment in Cases of Impeachment shall not extend further than to removal from Office, and disqualification to hold and enjoy any Office of honor, Trust or Profit under the United States: but the Party convicted shall nevertheless be liable and subject to Indictment, Trial, Judgment and Punishment, according to Law.

Section. 4.

The Times, Places and Manner of holding Elections for Senators and Representatives, shall be prescribed in each State by the Legislature thereof; but the Congress may at any time by Law make or alter such Regulations, except as to the Places of chusing Senators.

The Congress shall assemble at least once in every Year, and such Meeting shall be on the first Monday in December, unless they shall by Law appoint a different Day.

Section. 5.

Each House shall be the Judge of the Elections, Returns and Qualifications of its own Members, and a Majority of each shall constitute a Quorum to do Business; but a smaller Number may adjourn from day to day, and may be authorized to compel the attendance of absent Members, in such Manner, and under such Penalties as each House may provide.
Each House may determine the Rules of its Proceedings, punish its Members for disorderly Behaviour, and, with the Concurrence of two thirds, expel a Member.
Each House shall keep a Journal of its Proceedings, and from time to time publish the same, excepting such Parts as may in their Judgment require Secrecy; and the Yeas and Nays of the Members of either House on any question shall, at the Desire of one fifth of those Present, be entered on the Journal.
Neither House, during the Session of Congress, shall, without the Consent of the other, adjourn for more than three days, nor to any other Place than that in which the two Houses shall be sitting.

Section. 6.

The Senators and Representatives shall receive a Compensation for their Services, to be ascertained by Law, and paid out of the Treasury of the United States. They shall in all Cases, except Treason,

Felony and Breach of the Peace, be privileged from Arrest during their Attendance at the Session of their respective Houses, and in going to and returning from the same; and for any Speech or Debate in either House, they shall not be questioned in any other Place.

No Senator or Representative shall, during the Time for which he was elected, be appointed to any civil Office under the Authority of the United States, which shall have been created, or the Emoluments whereof shall have been encreased during such time; and no Person holding any Office under the United States, shall be a Member of either House during his Continuance in Office.

Section. 7.

All Bills for raising Revenue shall originate in the House of Representatives; but the Senate may propose or concur with Amendments as on other Bills.

Every Bill which shall have passed the House of Representatives and the Senate, shall, before it become a Law, be presented to the President of the United States; If he approve he shall sign it, but if not he shall return it, with his Objections to that House in which it shall have originated, who shall enter the Objections at large on their Journal, and proceed to reconsider it. If after such Reconsideration two thirds of that House shall agree to pass the Bill, it shall be sent, together with the Objections, to the other House, by which it shall likewise be reconsidered, and if approved by two thirds of that House, it shall become a Law. But in all such Cases the Votes of both Houses shall be determined by yeas and Nays, and the Names of the Persons voting for and against the Bill shall be entered on the Journal of each House respectively. If any Bill shall not be returned by the President within ten Days (Sundays excepted) after it shall have been presented to him, the Same shall be a Law, in like Manner as if he had signed it, unless the Congress by their Adjournment prevent its Return, in which Case it shall not be a Law.

Every Order, Resolution, or Vote to which the Concurrence of the Senate and House of Representatives may be necessary (except on a question of Adjournment) shall be presented to the President of the United States; and before the Same shall take Effect, shall be approved by him, or being disapproved by him, shall be repassed by two thirds of the Senate and House of Representatives, according to the Rules and Limitations prescribed in the Case of a Bill.

Section. 8.

The Congress shall have Power To lay and collect Taxes, Duties, Imposts and Excises, to pay the Debts and provide for the common Defence and general Welfare of the United States; but all Duties,

Imposts and Excises shall be uniform throughout the United States;
To borrow Money on the credit of the United States;
To regulate Commerce with foreign Nations, and among the several States, and with the Indian Tribes;
To establish an uniform Rule of Naturalization, and uniform Laws on the subject of Bankruptcies throughout the United States;
To coin Money, regulate the Value thereof, and of foreign Coin, and fix the Standard of Weights and Measures;
To provide for the Punishment of counterfeiting the Securities and current Coin of the United States;
To establish Post Offices and post Roads;
To promote the Progress of Science and useful Arts, by securing for limited Times to Authors and Inventors the exclusive Right to their respective Writings and Discoveries;
To constitute Tribunals inferior to the supreme Court;
To define and punish Piracies and Felonies committed on the high Seas, and Offences against the Law of Nations;
To declare War, grant Letters of Marque and Reprisal, and make Rules concerning Captures on Land and Water;
To raise and support Armies, but no Appropriation of Money to that Use shall be for a longer Term than two Years;
To provide and maintain a Navy;

To make Rules for the Government and Regulation of the land and naval Forces;

To provide for calling forth the Militia to execute the Laws of the Union, suppress Insurrections and repel Invasions;

To provide for organizing, arming, and disciplining, the Militia, and for governing such Part of them as may be employed in the Service of the United States, reserving to the States respectively, the Appointment of the Officers, and the Authority of training the Militia according to the discipline prescribed by Congress;

To exercise exclusive Legislation in all Cases whatsoever, over such District (not exceeding ten Miles square) as may, by Cession of particular States, and the Acceptance of Congress, become the Seat of the Government of the United States, and to exercise like Authority over all Places purchased by the Consent of the Legislature of the State in which the Same shall be, for the Erection of Forts, Magazines, Arsenals, dock-Yards, and other needful Buildings;—And

To make all Laws which shall be necessary and proper for carrying into Execution the foregoing Powers, and all other Powers vested by this Constitution in the Government of the United States, or in any Department or Officer thereof.

Section. 9.

The Migration or Importation of such Persons as any of the States now existing shall think proper to admit, shall not be prohibited by the Congress prior to the Year one thousand eight hundred and eight, but a Tax or duty may be imposed on such Importation, not exceeding ten dollars for each Person.

The Privilege of the Writ of Habeas Corpus shall not be suspended, unless when in Cases of Rebellion or Invasion the public Safety may require it.

No Bill of Attainder or ex post facto Law shall be passed.

No Capitation, or other direct, Tax shall be laid, unless in Proportion to the Census or enumeration herein before directed to be taken.

No Tax or Duty shall be laid on Articles exported from any State.

No Preference shall be given by any Regulation of Commerce or Revenue to the Ports of one State over those of another: nor shall Vessels bound to, or from, one State, be obliged to enter, clear, or pay Duties in another.

No Money shall be drawn from the Treasury, but in Consequence of Appropriations made by Law; and a regular Statement and Account of the Receipts and Expenditures of all public Money shall be published from time to time.

No Title of Nobility shall be granted by the United States: And no Person holding any Office of Profit or Trust under them, shall, without the Consent of the Congress, accept of any present, Emolument,

Office, or Title, of any kind whatever, from any King, Prince, or foreign State.

Section. 10.

No State shall enter into any Treaty, Alliance, or Confederation; grant Letters of Marque and Reprisal; coin Money; emit Bills of Credit; make any Thing but gold and silver Coin a Tender in Payment of Debts; pass any Bill of Attainder, ex post facto Law, or Law impairing the Obligation of Contracts, or grant any Title of Nobility.
No State shall, without the Consent of the Congress, lay any Imposts or Duties on Imports or Exports, except what may be absolutely necessary for executing it's inspection Laws: and the net Produce of all Duties and Imposts, laid by any State on Imports or Exports, shall be for the Use of the Treasury of the United States; and all such Laws shall be subject to the Revision and Controul of the Congress.
No State shall, without the Consent of Congress, lay any Duty of Tonnage, keep Troops, or Ships of War in time of Peace, enter into any Agreement or Compact with another State, or with a foreign Power, or engage in War, unless actually invaded, or in such imminent Danger as will not admit of delay.

Article. II.

Section. 1.

The executive Power shall be vested in a President of the United States of America. He shall hold his Office during the Term of four Years, and, together with the Vice President, chosen for the same Term, be elected, as follows:

Each State shall appoint, in such Manner as the Legislature thereof may direct, a Number of Electors, equal to the whole Number of Senators and Representatives to which the State may be entitled in the Congress: but no Senator or Representative, or Person holding an Office of Trust or Profit under the United States, shall be appointed an Elector.

The Electors shall meet in their respective States, and vote by Ballot for two Persons, of whom one at least shall not be an inhabitant of the same State with themselves. And they shall make a List of all the Persons voted for, and of the Number of Votes for each; which list they shall sign and certify, and transmit sealed to the Seat of the Government of the United States, directed to the President of the Senate. The President of the Senate shall, in the Presence of the Senate and House of Representatives, open all the Certificates, and the Votes shall then be counted. The Person having the greatest Number of Votes shall be the President, if such Number be a Majority of the whole Number of Electors appointed; and if there be more than one who have such Majority, and have an equal Number of Votes, then the House of Representatives shall immediately chuse by Ballot one of them for

President; and if no Person have a Majority, then from the five highest on the List the said House shall in like Manner chuse the President. But in chusing the President, the Votes shall be taken by States, the Representation from each State having one Vote; A quorum for this Purpose shall consist of a Member or Members from two thirds of the States, and a Majority of all the States shall be necessary to a Choice. In every Case, after the Choice of President, the Person having the greatest Number of Votes of the Electors shall be the Vice President. But if there should remain two or more who have equal Votes, the Senate shall chuse from them by Ballot the Vice President.

The Congress may determine the Time of chusing the Electors, and the Day on which they shall give their Votes; which Day shall be the same throughout the United States.

No Person except a natural born Citizen, or a Citizen of the United States, at the time of the Adoption of this Constitution, shall be eligible to the Office of President; neither shall any Person be eligible to that Office who shall not have attained to the Age of thirty five Years, and been fourteen Years a Resident within the United States.

In Case of the Removal of the President from Office, or of his Death, Resignation, or Inability to discharge the Powers and Duties of the said Office, the Same shall devolve on the Vice President, and the Congress may by Law provide for the Case of Removal, Death, Resignation or Inability, both of the President and Vice President, declaring what Officer shall then act as President, and such Officer shall act accordingly, until the Disability be removed, or a President shall be elected.

The President shall, at stated Times, receive for his Services, a Compensation, which shall neither be encreased nor diminished during the Period for which he shall have been elected, and he shall not receive within that Period any other Emolument from the United States, or any of them.

Before he enter on the Execution of his Office, he shall take the following Oath or Affirmation:—"I do solemnly swear (or affirm) that I will faithfully execute the Office of President of the United States, and will to the best of my Ability, preserve, protect and defend the Constitution of the United States."

Section. 2.

The President shall be Commander in Chief of the Army and Navy of the United States, and of the Militia of the several States, when called into the actual Service of the United States; he may require the Opinion, in writing, of the principal Officer in each of the executive Departments, upon any Subject relating to the Duties of their respective Offices, and he shall have Power to grant Reprieves and Pardons for Offences against the United States, except in Cases of Impeachment.

He shall have Power, by and with the Advice and Consent of the Senate, to make Treaties, provided two thirds of the Senators present concur; and he shall nominate, and by and with the Advice and Consent of the Senate, shall appoint Ambassadors, other public Ministers and Consuls, Judges of the supreme Court, and all other Officers of the United States, whose Appointments are not herein otherwise provided for, and which shall be established by Law: but the Congress may by Law vest the Appointment of such inferior Officers, as they think proper, in the President alone, in the Courts of Law, or in the Heads of Departments.

The President shall have Power to fill up all Vacancies that may happen during the Recess of the Senate, by granting Commissions which shall expire at the End of their next Session.

Section. 3.

He shall from time to time give to the Congress Information of the State of the Union, and recommend to their Consideration such Measures as he shall judge necessary and expedient; he may, on extraordinary Occasions, convene both Houses, or either of them, and in Case of Disagreement between them, with Respect to the Time of Adjournment, he may adjourn them to such Time as he shall think proper; he shall receive Ambassadors and other public Ministers; he shall take Care that the Laws be faithfully executed, and shall Commission all the Officers of the United States.

Section. 4.

The President, Vice President and all civil Officers of the United States, shall be removed from Office on Impeachment for, and Conviction of, Treason, Bribery, or other high Crimes and Misdemeanors.
Article III.

Section. 1.

The judicial Power of the United States, shall be vested in one supreme Court, and in such inferior Courts as the Congress may from time to time ordain and establish. The Judges, both of the supreme and inferior Courts, shall hold their Offices during good Behaviour, and shall, at stated Times, receive for their Services, a Compensation, which shall not be diminished during their Continuance in Office.

Section. 2.

The judicial Power shall extend to all Cases, in Law and Equity, arising under this Constitution, the Laws of the United States, and Treaties made, or which shall be made, under their Authority;—to all Cases affecting Ambassadors, other public Ministers and Consuls;—to all Cases of admiralty and maritime Jurisdiction;—to Controversies to which the United States shall be a Party;—to Controversies between

two or more States;— between a State and Citizens of another State,—between Citizens of different States,—between Citizens of the same State claiming Lands under Grants of different States, and between a State, or the Citizens thereof, and foreign States, Citizens or Subjects.
In all Cases affecting Ambassadors, other public Ministers and Consuls, and those in which a State shall be Party, the supreme Court shall have original Jurisdiction. In all the other Cases before mentioned, the supreme Court shall have appellate Jurisdiction, both as to Law and Fact, with such Exceptions, and under such Regulations as the Congress shall make.
The Trial of all Crimes, except in Cases of Impeachment, shall be by Jury; and such Trial shall be held in the State where the said Crimes shall have been committed; but when not committed within any State, the Trial shall be at such Place or Places as the Congress may by Law have directed.

Section. 3.

Treason against the United States, shall consist only in levying War against them, or in adhering to their Enemies, giving them Aid and Comfort. No Person shall be convicted of Treason unless on the Testimony of two Witnesses to the same overt Act, or on Confession in open Court.
The Congress shall have Power to declare the Punishment of Treason, but no Attainder of Treason

shall work Corruption of Blood, or Forfeiture except during the Life of the Person attainted.

Article. IV.

Section. 1.

Full Faith and Credit shall be given in each State to the public Acts, Records, and judicial Proceedings of every other State. And the Congress may by general Laws prescribe the Manner in which such Acts, Records and Proceedings shall be proved, and the Effect thereof.

Section. 2.

The Citizens of each State shall be entitled to all Privileges and Immunities of Citizens in the several States.

A Person charged in any State with Treason, Felony, or other Crime, who shall flee from Justice, and be found in another State, shall on Demand of the executive Authority of the State from which he fled, be delivered up, to be removed to the State having Jurisdiction of the Crime.

No Person held to Service or Labour in one State, under the Laws thereof, escaping into another, shall, in Consequence of any Law or Regulation therein, be discharged from such Service or Labour, but shall be delivered up on Claim of the Party to whom such Service or Labour may be due.

Section. 3.

New States may be admitted by the Congress into this Union; but no new State shall be formed or erected within the Jurisdiction of any other State; nor any State be formed by the Junction of two or more States, or Parts of States, without the Consent of the Legislatures of the States concerned as well as of the Congress.

The Congress shall have Power to dispose of and make all needful Rules and Regulations respecting the Territory or other Property belonging to the United States; and nothing in this Constitution shall be so construed as to Prejudice any Claims of the United States, or of any particular State.

Section. 4.

The United States shall guarantee to every State in this Union a Republican Form of Government, and shall protect each of them against Invasion; and on Application of the Legislature, or of the Executive (when the Legislature cannot be convened), against domestic Violence.

Article. V.

The Congress, whenever two thirds of both Houses shall deem it necessary, shall propose Amendments to this Constitution, or, on the Application of the

Legislatures of two thirds of the several States, shall call a Convention for proposing Amendments, which, in either Case, shall be valid to all Intents and Purposes, as Part of this Constitution, when ratified by the Legislatures of three fourths of the several States, or by Conventions in three fourths thereof, as the one or the other Mode of Ratification may be proposed by the Congress; Provided that no Amendment which may be made prior to the Year One thousand eight hundred and eight shall in any Manner affect the first and fourth Clauses in the Ninth Section of the first Article; and that no State, without its Consent, shall be deprived of its equal Suffrage in the Senate.

Article. VI.

All Debts contracted and Engagements entered into, before the Adoption of this Constitution, shall be as valid against the United States under this Constitution, as under the Confederation.
This Constitution, and the Laws of the United States which shall be made in Pursuance thereof; and all Treaties made, or which shall be made, under the Authority of the United States, shall be the supreme Law of the Land; and the Judges in every State shall be bound thereby, any Thing in the Constitution or Laws of any State to the Contrary notwithstanding.
The Senators and Representatives before mentioned, and the Members of the several State Legislatures, and all executive and judicial Officers, both of the

United States and of the several States, shall be bound by Oath or Affirmation, to support this Constitution; but no religious Test shall ever be required as a Qualification to any Office or public Trust under the United States.

Article. VII.

The Ratification of the Conventions of nine States, shall be sufficient for the Establishment of this Constitution between the States so ratifying the Same.
The Word, "the," being interlined between the seventh and eighth Lines of the first Page, The Word "Thirty" being partly written on an Erazure in the fifteenth Line of the first Page, The Words "is tried" being interlined between the thirty second and thirty third Lines of the first Page and the Word "the" being interlined between the forty third and forty fourth Lines of the second Page.

Done in Convention by the Unanimous Consent of the States present the Seventeenth Day of September in the Year of our Lord one thousand seven hundred and Eighty seven and of the Independence of the United States of America the Twelfth In witness whereof We have hereunto subscribed our Names,

GEORGE WASHINGTON,
President, and Deputy from Virginia

NEW HAMPSHIRE
John Langdon, Nicholas Gilman

MASSACHUSETTS
Nathaniel Gorman, Rufus King

NEW JERSEY
William Livingston, David Brearly, William Patterson, Jonathan Dayton

CONNECTICUT
William Samuel Johnson, Roger Sherman

NEW YORK
Alexander Hamilton

MARYLAND
James McHenry, Daniel of St. Tho. Jenifer, Daniel Carroll

VIRGINIA
John Blair, James Madison, jun

PENNSYLVANIA
Benjamin Franklin, Thomas Mifflin, Robert Morris, George Clymer, Thomas Fitz Simons, Jared Ingersoll, James Wilson, Governuer Morris

DELAWARE

George Read, Gunning Bedford, jun. John Dickinson, Richard Bassett, Jacob Broom

NORTH CAROLINA
William Blunt, Richard Dobbs Spaight, Hugh Williamson

SOUTH CAROLINA
John Rutledge, Chas. Cotesworth Pinckney, Pierce Butler

GEORGIA
William Few, Abraham Baldwin

AMENDMENT I

Congress shall make no law respecting an establishment of religion, or prohibiting the free exercise thereof; or abridging the freedom of speech, or of the press; or the right of the people peaceably to assemble, and to petition the Government for a redress of grievances.

AMENDMENT II

A well regulated Militia, being necessary to the security of a free State, the right of the people to keep and bear Arms, shall not be infringed.

AMENDMENT III

No Soldier shall, in time of peace be quartered in any house, without the consent of the Owner, nor in time of war, but in a manner to be prescribed by law.

AMENDMENT IV

The right of the people to be secure in their persons, houses, papers, and effects, against unreasonable searches and seizures, shall not be violated, and no Warrants shall issue, but upon probable cause, supported by Oath or affirmation, and particularly describing the place to be searched, and the persons or things to be seized.

AMENDMENT V

No person shall be held to answer for a capital, or otherwise infamous crime, unless on a presentment or indictment of a Grand Jury, except in cases arising in the land or naval forces, or in the Militia, when in actual service in time of War or public danger; nor shall any person be subject for the same offence to be twice put in jeopardy of life or limb; nor shall be compelled in any criminal case to be a witness against himself, nor be deprived of life, liberty, or property, without due process of law; nor shall private property be taken for public use, without just compensation.

AMENDMENT VI

In all criminal prosecutions, the accused shall enjoy the right to a speedy and public trial, by an impartial jury of the State and district wherein the crime shall have been committed, which district shall have been previously ascertained by law, and to be informed of the nature and cause of the accusation; to be confronted with the witnesses against him; to have compulsory process for obtaining witnesses in his favor, and to have the Assistance of Counsel for his defence.

AMENDMENT VII

In Suits at common law, where the value in controversy shall exceed twenty dollars, the right of trial by jury shall be preserved, and no fact tried by a jury, shall be otherwise re-examined in any Court of the United States, than according to the rules of the common law.

AMENDMENT VIII

Excessive bail shall not be required, nor excessive fines imposed, nor cruel and unusual punishments inflicted.

AMENDMENT IX

The enumeration in the Constitution, of certain rights, shall not be construed to deny or disparage others retained by the people.

AMENDMENT X

The powers not delegated to the United States by the Constitution, nor prohibited by it to the States, are reserved to the States respectively, or to the people.

AMENDMENT XI

Passed by Congress March 4, 1794. Ratified February 7, 1795.
Note: Article III, section 2, of the Constitution was modified by amendment 11.
The Judicial power of the United States shall not be construed to extend to any suit in law or equity, commenced or prosecuted against one of the United States by Citizens of another State, or by Citizens or Subjects of any Foreign State.

AMENDMENT XII

Passed by Congress December 9, 1803. Ratified June 15, 1804.
Note: A portion of Article II, section 1 of the Constitution was superseded by the 12th amendment.

The Electors shall meet in their respective states and vote by ballot for President and Vice-President, one of whom, at least, shall not be an inhabitant of the same state with themselves; they shall name in their ballots the person voted for as President, and in distinct ballots the person voted for as Vice-President, and they shall make distinct lists of all persons voted for as President, and of all persons voted for as Vice-President, and of the number of votes for each, which lists they shall sign and certify, and transmit sealed to the seat of the government of the United States, directed to the President of the Senate; -- the President of the Senate shall, in the presence of the Senate and House of Representatives, open all the certificates and the votes shall then be counted; -- The person having the greatest number of votes for President, shall be the President, if such number be a majority of the whole number of Electors appointed; and if no person have such majority, then from the persons having the highest numbers not exceeding three on the list of those voted for as President, the House of Representatives shall choose immediately, by ballot, the President. But in choosing the President, the votes shall be taken by states, the representation from each state having one vote; a quorum for this purpose shall consist of a member or members from two-thirds of the states, and a majority of all the states shall be necessary to a choice. [And if the House of Representatives shall not choose a President whenever the right of choice shall devolve upon them, before the fourth day of March next following, then the Vice-President shall act as President, as in case of the death or other constitutional disability of the President. --]* The person having the greatest number of votes as Vice-President, shall be the Vice-President, if such number be a majority of the whole number of Electors appointed, and if no person have a majority, then from the two highest numbers on the list, the Senate shall choose the Vice-President; a quorum for the purpose shall consist of two-thirds of the whole number of Senators, and a majority of the whole number shall be necessary to a choice. But no person constitutionally ineligible to the office of President shall be eligible to that of Vice-President of the United States. *Superseded by section 3 of the 20th amendment.

AMENDMENT XIII

Passed by Congress January 31, 1865. Ratified December 6, 1865.
Note: A portion of Article IV, section 2, of the Constitution was superseded by the 13th amendment.

Section 1.

Neither slavery nor involuntary servitude, except as a punishment for crime whereof the party shall have been duly convicted, shall exist within the United States, or any place subject to their jurisdiction.

Section 2.

Congress shall have power to enforce this article by appropriate legislation.

AMENDMENT XIV

Passed by Congress June 13, 1866. Ratified July 9, 1868.
Note: Article I, section 2, of the Constitution was modified by section 2 of the 14th amendment.

Section 1.

All persons born or naturalized in the United States, and subject to the jurisdiction thereof, are citizens of the United States and of the State wherein they reside. No State shall make or enforce any law which shall abridge the privileges or immunities of citizens of the United States; nor shall any State deprive any person of life, liberty, or property, without due process of law; nor deny to any person within its jurisdiction the equal protection of the laws.

Section 2.

Representatives shall be apportioned among the several States according to their respective numbers, counting the whole number of persons in each State, excluding Indians not taxed. But when the right to vote at any election for the choice of electors for President and Vice-President of the United States, Representatives in Congress, the Executive and Judicial officers of a State, or the members of the Legislature thereof, is denied to any of the male inhabitants of such State, being twenty-one years of age,* and citizens of the United States, or in any way abridged, except for participation in rebellion, or other crime, the basis of representation therein shall be reduced in the proportion which the number of such male citizens shall bear to the whole number of male citizens twenty-one years of age in such State.

Section 3.

No person shall be a Senator or Representative in Congress, or elector of President and Vice-President, or hold any office, civil or military, under the United States, or under any State, who, having previously taken an oath, as a member of Congress, or as an officer of the United States, or as a member of any State legislature, or as an executive or judicial officer of any State, to support the Constitution of the United States, shall have engaged in insurrection or rebellion against the same, or given aid or comfort to the enemies thereof. But Congress may by a vote of two-thirds of each House, remove such disability.

Section 4.

The validity of the public debt of the United States, authorized by law, including debts incurred for payment of pensions and bounties for services in suppressing insurrection or rebellion, shall not be questioned. But neither the United States nor any State shall assume or pay any debt or obligation incurred in aid of insurrection or rebellion against the United States, or any claim for the loss or emancipation of any slave; but all such debts, obligations and claims shall be held illegal and void.

Section 5.

The Congress shall have the power to enforce, by appropriate legislation, the provisions of this article.
*Changed by section 1 of the 26th amendment.

AMENDMENT XV

Passed by Congress February 26, 1869. Ratified February 3, 1870.

Section 1.

The right of citizens of the United States to vote shall not be denied or abridged by the United States or by any State on account of race, color, or previous condition of servitude.

Section 2.

The Congress shall have the power to enforce this article by appropriate legislation.

AMENDMENT XVI

Passed by Congress July 2, 1909. Ratified February 3, 1913.
Note: Article I, section 9, of the Constitution was modified by amendment 16.
The Congress shall have power to lay and collect taxes on incomes, from whatever source derived, without apportionment among the several States, and without regard to any census or enumeration.

AMENDMENT XVII

Passed by Congress May 13, 1912. Ratified April 8, 1913.
Note: Article I, section 3, of the Constitution was modified by the 17th amendment.
The Senate of the United States shall be composed of two Senators from each State, elected by the

people thereof, for six years; and each Senator shall have one vote. The electors in each State shall have the qualifications requisite for electors of the most numerous branch of the State legislatures.

When vacancies happen in the representation of any State in the Senate, the executive authority of such State shall issue writs of election to fill such vacancies: Provided, That the legislature of any State may empower the executive thereof to make temporary appointments until the people fill the vacancies by election as the legislature may direct.

This amendment shall not be so construed as to affect the election or term of any Senator chosen before it becomes valid as part of the Constitution.

AMENDMENT XVIII

Passed by Congress December 18, 1917. Ratified January 16, 1919. Repealed by amendment 21.

Section 1.

After one year from the ratification of this article the manufacture, sale, or transportation of intoxicating liquors within, the importation thereof into, or the exportation thereof from the United States and all territory subject to the jurisdiction thereof for beverage purposes is hereby prohibited.

Section 2.

The Congress and the several States shall have concurrent power to enforce this article by appropriate legislation.

Section 3.

This article shall be inoperative unless it shall have been ratified as an amendment to the Constitution by the legislatures of the several States, as provided in the Constitution, within seven years from the date of the submission hereof to the States by the Congress.

AMENDMENT XIX

Passed by Congress June 4, 1919. Ratified August 18, 1920.
The right of citizens of the United States to vote shall not be denied or abridged by the United States or by any State on account of sex.
Congress shall have power to enforce this article by appropriate legislation.

AMENDMENT XX

Passed by Congress March 2, 1932. Ratified January 23, 1933.
Note: Article I, section 4, of the Constitution was modified by section 2 of this amendment. In

addition, a portion of the 12th amendment was superseded by section 3.

Section 1.

The terms of the President and the Vice President shall end at noon on the 20th day of January, and the terms of Senators and Representatives at noon on the 3d day of January, of the years in which such terms would have ended if this article had not been ratified; and the terms of their successors shall then begin.

Section 2.

The Congress shall assemble at least once in every year, and such meeting shall begin at noon on the 3d day of January, unless they shall by law appoint a different day.

Section 3.

If, at the time fixed for the beginning of the term of the President, the President elect shall have died, the Vice President elect shall become President. If a President shall not have been chosen before the time fixed for the beginning of his term, or if the President elect shall have failed to qualify, then the Vice President elect shall act as President until a President shall have qualified; and the Congress may by law provide for the case wherein neither a

President elect nor a Vice President elect shall have qualified, declaring who shall then act as President, or the manner in which one who is to act shall be selected, and such person shall act accordingly until a President or Vice President shall have qualified.

Section 4.

The Congress may by law provide for the case of the death of any of the persons from whom the House of Representatives may choose a President whenever the right of choice shall have devolved upon them, and for the case of the death of any of the persons from whom the Senate may choose a Vice President whenever the right of choice shall have devolved upon them.

Section 5.

Sections 1 and 2 shall take effect on the 15th day of October following the ratification of this article.
Section 6.

This article shall be inoperative unless it shall have been ratified as an amendment to the Constitution by the legislatures of three-fourths of the several States within seven years from the date of its submission.

AMENDMENT XXI

Passed by Congress February 20, 1933. Ratified December 5, 1933.

Section 1.

The eighteenth article of amendment to the Constitution of the United States is hereby repealed.

Section 2.

The transportation or importation into any State, Territory, or possession of the United States for delivery or use therein of intoxicating liquors, in violation of the laws thereof, is hereby prohibited.
Section 3.

This article shall be inoperative unless it shall have been ratified as an amendment to the Constitution by conventions in the several States, as provided in the Constitution, within seven years from the date of the submission hereof to the States by the Congress.

AMENDMENT XXII

Passed by Congress March 21, 1947. Ratified February 27, 1951.

Section 1.

No person shall be elected to the office of the President more than twice, and no person who has held the office of President, or acted as President, for more than two years of a term to which some other person was elected President shall be elected to the office of the President more than once. But this Article shall not apply to any person holding the office of President when this Article was proposed by the Congress, and shall not prevent any person who may be holding the office of President, or acting as President, during the term within which this Article becomes operative from holding the office of President or acting as President during the remainder of such term.

Section 2.

This article shall be inoperative unless it shall have been ratified as an amendment to the Constitution by the legislatures of three-fourths of the several States within seven years from the date of its submission to the States by the Congress.

AMENDMENT XXIII

Passed by Congress June 16, 1960. Ratified March 29, 1961.

Section 1.

The District constituting the seat of Government of the United States shall appoint in such manner as the Congress may direct:
A number of electors of President and Vice President equal to the whole number of Senators and Representatives in Congress to which the District would be entitled if it were a State, but in no event more than the least populous State; they shall be in addition to those appointed by the States, but they shall be considered, for the purposes of the election of President and Vice President, to be electors appointed by a State; and they shall meet in the District and perform such duties as provided by the twelfth article of amendment.

Section 2.

The Congress shall have power to enforce this article by appropriate legislation.

AMENDMENT XXIV

Passed by Congress August 27, 1962. Ratified January 23, 1964.

Section 1.

The right of citizens of the United States to vote in any primary or other election for President or Vice President, for electors for President or Vice President, or for Senator or Representative in

Congress, shall not be denied or abridged by the United States or any State by reason of failure to pay any poll tax or other tax.

Section 2.

The Congress shall have power to enforce this article by appropriate legislation.

AMENDMENT XXV

Passed by Congress July 6, 1965. Ratified February 10, 1967.
Note: Article II, section 1, of the Constitution was affected by the 25th amendment.

Section 1.

In case of the removal of the President from office or of his death or resignation, the Vice President shall become President.

Section 2.

Whenever there is a vacancy in the office of the Vice President, the President shall nominate a Vice President who shall take office upon confirmation by a majority vote of both Houses of Congress.

Section 3.

Whenever the President transmits to the President pro tempore of the Senate and the Speaker of the House of Representatives his written declaration that he is unable to discharge the powers and duties of his office, and until he transmits to them a written declaration to the contrary, such powers and duties shall be discharged by the Vice President as Acting President.

Section 4.

Whenever the Vice President and a majority of either the principal officers of the executive departments or of such other body as Congress may by law provide, transmit to the President pro tempore of the Senate and the Speaker of the House of Representatives their written declaration that the President is unable to discharge the powers and duties of his office, the Vice President shall immediately assume the powers and duties of the office as Acting President.

Thereafter, when the President transmits to the President pro tempore of the Senate and the Speaker of the House of Representatives his written declaration that no inability exists, he shall resume the powers and duties of his office unless the Vice President and a majority of either the principal officers of the executive department or of such other body as Congress may by law provide, transmit within four days to the President pro tempore of the Senate and the Speaker of the House of

Representatives their written declaration that the President is unable to discharge the powers and duties of his office. Thereupon Congress shall decide the issue, assembling within forty-eight hours for that purpose if not in session. If the Congress, within twenty-one days after receipt of the latter written declaration, or, if Congress is not in session, within twenty-one days after Congress is required to assemble, determines by two-thirds vote of both Houses that the President is unable to discharge the powers and duties of his office, the Vice President shall continue to discharge the same as Acting President; otherwise, the President shall resume the powers and duties of his office.

AMENDMENT XXVI

Passed by Congress March 23, 1971. Ratified July 1, 1971.
Note: Amendment 14, section 2, of the Constitution was modified by section 1 of the 26th amendment.

Section 1.

The right of citizens of the United States, who are eighteen years of age or older, to vote shall not be denied or abridged by the United States or by any State on account of age.

Section 2.

The Congress shall have power to enforce this article by appropriate legislation.

AMENDMENT XXVII

Originally proposed Sept. 25, 1789. Ratified May 7, 1992.
No law, varying the compensation for the services of the Senators and Representatives, shall take effect, until an election of Representatives shall have intervened.

WOODROW POLSTON

The Declaration of Independence

In Congress, July 4, 1776
The unanimous Declaration of the thirteen united States of America, When in the Course of human events, it becomes necessary for one people to dissolve the political bands which have connected them with another, and to assume among the powers of the earth, the separate and equal station to which the Laws of Nature and of Nature's God entitle them, a decent respect to the opinions of mankind requires that they should declare the causes which impel them to the separation.

We hold these truths to be self-evident, that all men are created equal, that they are endowed by their Creator with certain unalienable Rights, that among these are Life, Liberty and the pursuit of Happiness.--That to secure these rights, Governments are instituted among Men, deriving their just powers from the consent of the governed, --That whenever any Form of Government becomes destructive of these ends, it is the Right of the People to alter or to abolish it, and to institute new Government, laying its foundation on such principles and organizing its powers in such form, as to them shall seem most likely to effect their Safety and Happiness. Prudence, indeed, will dictate that Governments long established should not be changed for light and transient causes; and accordingly all experience hath shewn, that mankind are more disposed to suffer, while evils are sufferable, than to right themselves by abolishing the forms to which they are accustomed. But when a long train of abuses and usurpations, pursuing invariably the same Object evinces a design to reduce them under absolute Despotism, it is their right, it is their duty, to throw off such Government, and to provide new Guards for their future security.--Such has been the patient sufferance of these Colonies; and such is now the necessity which constrains them to alter their former Systems of Government. The history of the present King of Great Britain is a history of repeated injuries and usurpations, all having in direct object the establishment of an absolute Tyranny over these States. To prove this, let Facts be submitted to a candid world.

He has refused his Assent to Laws, the most wholesome and necessary for the public good.

He has forbidden his Governors to pass Laws of immediate and pressing importance, unless suspended in their operation till his Assent should be obtained; and when so suspended, he has utterly neglected to attend to them.

He has refused to pass other Laws for the accommodation of large districts of people, unless those people would relinquish the right of Representation in the Legislature, a right inestimable to them and formidable to tyrants only.

He has called together legislative bodies at places unusual, uncomfortable, and distant from the depository of their public Records, for the sole purpose of fatiguing them into compliance with his measures.

He has dissolved Representative Houses repeatedly, for opposing with manly firmness his invasions on the rights of the people.

He has refused for a long time, after such dissolutions, to cause others to be elected; whereby the Legislative powers, incapable of Annihilation, have returned to the People at large for their exercise; the State remaining in the mean time exposed to all the dangers of invasion from without, and convulsions within.

He has endeavoured to prevent the population of these States; for that purpose obstructing the Laws for Naturalization of Foreigners; refusing to pass others to encourage their migrations hither, and raising the conditions of new Appropriations of Lands.

He has obstructed the Administration of Justice, by refusing his Assent to Laws for establishing Judiciary powers.

He has made Judges dependent on his Will alone, for the tenure of their offices, and the amount and payment of their salaries.

He has erected a multitude of New Offices, and sent hither swarms of Officers to harrass our people, and eat out their substance.

He has kept among us, in times of peace, Standing Armies without the Consent of our legislatures.

He has affected to render the Military independent of and superior to the Civil power.

He has combined with others to subject us to a jurisdiction foreign to our constitution, and unacknowledged by our laws; giving his Assent to their Acts of pretended Legislation:

For Quartering large bodies of armed troops among us:

For protecting them, by a mock Trial, from punishment for any Murders which they should commit on the Inhabitants of these States:

For cutting off our Trade with all parts of the world:

For imposing Taxes on us without our Consent:

For depriving us in many cases, of the benefits of Trial by Jury:

For transporting us beyond Seas to be tried for pretended offences

For abolishing the free System of English Laws in a neighbouring Province, establishing therein an Arbitrary government, and enlarging its Boundaries so as to render it at once an example and fit instrument for introducing the same absolute rule into these Colonies:

For taking away our Charters, abolishing our most valuable Laws, and altering fundamentally the Forms of our Governments:

For suspending our own Legislatures, and declaring themselves invested with power to legislate for us in all cases whatsoever.

He has abdicated Government here, by declaring us out of his Protection and waging War against us.

He has plundered our seas, ravaged our Coasts, burnt our towns, and destroyed the lives of our people.

He is at this time transporting large Armies of foreign Mercenaries to compleat the works of death, desolation and tyranny, already begun with circumstances of Cruelty & perfidy scarcely paralleled in the most barbarous ages, and totally unworthy the Head of a civilized nation.

He has constrained our fellow Citizens taken Captive on the high Seas to bear Arms against their Country, to become the executioners of their friends and Brethren, or to fall themselves by their Hands.

He has excited domestic insurrections amongst us, and has endeavoured to bring on the inhabitants of our frontiers, the merciless Indian Savages, whose known rule of warfare, is an undistinguished destruction of all ages, sexes and conditions.

In every stage of these Oppressions We have Petitioned for Redress in the most humble terms: Our repeated Petitions have been answered only by repeated injury. A Prince whose character is thus marked by every act which may define a Tyrant, is unfit to be the ruler of a free people.

Nor have We been wanting in attentions to our Brittish brethren. We have warned them from time to time of attempts by their legislature to extend an unwarrantable jurisdiction over us. We have reminded them of the circumstances of our emigration and settlement here. We have appealed to their native justice and magnanimity, and we have conjured them by the ties of our common kindred to disavow these usurpations, which, would inevitably interrupt our connections and correspondence. They too have been deaf to the voice of justice and of consanguinity. We must, therefore, acquiesce in the necessity, which denounces our Separation, and hold them, as we hold the rest of mankind, Enemies in War, in Peace Friends.

We, therefore, the Representatives of the united States of America, in General Congress, Assembled, appealing to the Supreme Judge of the world for the rectitude of our intentions, do, in the Name, and by Authority of the good People of these Colonies, solemnly publish and declare, That these United Colonies are, and of Right ought to be Free and Independent States; that they are Absolved from all Allegiance to the British Crown, and that all political connection between them and the State of Great Britain, is and ought to be totally dissolved; and that as Free and Independent States, they have full Power to levy War, conclude Peace, contract Alliances, establish Commerce, and to do all other Acts and Things which Independent States may of right do. And for the support of this Declaration, with a firm reliance on the protection of divine Providence, we mutually pledge to each other our Lives, our Fortunes and our sacred Honor.

AN AMERICAN HISTORY: OUR FOUNDATION AND MORAL COMPASS

Give Me Liberty Or Give Me Death

By

Patrick Henry

No man thinks more highly than I do of the patriotism, as well as abilities, of the very worthy gentlemen who have just addressed the House. But different men often see the same subject in different lights; and, therefore, I hope it will not be thought disrespectful to those gentlemen if, entertaining as I do opinions of a character very opposite to theirs, I shall speak forth my sentiments freely and without reserve. This is no time for ceremony. The question before the House is one of awful moment to this country. For my own part, I consider it as nothing less than a question of freedom or slavery; and in proportion to the magnitude of the subject ought to be the freedom of the debate. It is only in this way that we can hope to arrive at truth, and fulfill the great responsibility which we hold to God and our country. Should I keep back my opinions at such a time, through fear of giving offense, I should consider myself as guilty of treason towards my country, and of an act of disloyalty toward the Majesty of Heaven, which I revere above all earthly kings.

Mr. President, it is natural to man to indulge in the illusions of hope. We are apt to shut our eyes against a painful truth, and listen to the song of that siren till she transforms us into beasts. Is this the part of wise men, engaged in a great and arduous struggle for liberty? Are we disposed to be of the number of those who, having eyes, see not, and, having ears, hear not, the things which so nearly concern their temporal salvation? For my part, whatever anguish of spirit it may cost, I am willing to know the whole truth; to know the worst, and to provide for it.

I have but one lamp by which my feet are guided, and that is the lamp of experience. I know of no way of judging of the future but by the past. And judging by the past, I wish to know what there has been in the conduct of the British ministry for the last ten years to justify those hopes with which gentlemen have been pleased to solace themselves and the House. Is it that insidious smile with which our petition has been lately received? Trust it not, sir; it will prove a snare to your feet. Suffer not yourselves to be betrayed with a kiss. Ask yourselves how this gracious reception of our petition comports with those warlike preparations which cover our waters and darken our land. Are fleets and armies necessary to a work of love and reconciliation? Have we shown ourselves so unwilling to be reconciled that force must be called in to win back our love? Let us not deceive ourselves, sir. These are the implements of war and subjugation; the last arguments to which kings resort. I ask gentlemen, sir, what means this martial array, if its purpose be not to force us to submission? Can gentlemen assign any other possible motive for it? Has Great Britain any enemy, in this quarter of the world, to call for all this accumulation of navies and armies? No, sir, she has none. They are meant for us: they can be meant for no other. They are sent over to bind and rivet upon us those chains which the British ministry have been so long forging. And what have we to oppose to them? Shall we try argument? Sir, we have been trying that for the last ten years. Have we anything new to offer upon the subject? Nothing. We have held the subject up in every light of which it is capable; but it has been all in vain. Shall we resort to entreaty and humble supplication? What terms shall we find which have not been already exhausted? Let us not, I beseech you, sir, deceive ourselves. Sir, we have done everything that could be done to avert the storm which is now coming on. We have petitioned; we have remonstrated; we have supplicated; we have prostrated ourselves before the throne, and have implored its interposition to arrest the tyrannical hands of the ministry and Parliament. Our petitions have been slighted; our remonstrances have produced additional violence and insult; our supplications have been disregarded; and we have been spurned, with contempt, from the foot of the throne! In vain, after these things, may we indulge the fond hope of peace and reconciliation. There is no longer any room for

hope. If we wish to be free-- if we mean to preserve inviolate those inestimable privileges for which we have been so long contending--if we mean not basely to abandon the noble struggle in which we have been so long engaged, and which we have pledged ourselves never to abandon until the glorious object of our contest shall be obtained--we must fight! I repeat it, sir, we must fight! An appeal to arms and to the God of hosts is all that is left us!
They tell us, sir, that we are weak; unable to cope with so formidable an adversary. But when shall we be stronger? Will it be the next week, or the next year? Will it be when we are totally disarmed, and when a British guard shall be stationed in every house? Shall we gather strength by irresolution and inaction? Shall we acquire the means of effectual resistance by lying supinely on our backs and hugging the delusive phantom of hope, until our enemies shall have bound us hand and foot? Sir, we are not weak if we make a proper use of those means which the God of nature hath placed in our power. The millions of people, armed in the holy cause of liberty, and in such a country as that which we possess, are invincible by any force which our enemy can send against us. Besides, sir, we shall not fight our battles alone. There is a just God who presides over the destinies of nations, and who will raise up friends to fight our battles for us. The battle, sir, is not to the strong alone; it is to the vigilant, the active, the brave. Besides, sir, we have no election. If we were base enough to desire it, it is

now too late to retire from the contest. There is no retreat but in submission and slavery! Our chains are forged! Their clanking may be heard on the plains of Boston! The war is inevitable--and let it come! I repeat it, sir, let it come.

It is in vain, sir, to extenuate the matter. Gentlemen may cry, Peace, Peace-- but there is no peace. The war is actually begun! The next gale that sweeps from the north will bring to our ears the clash of resounding arms! Our brethren are already in the field! Why stand we here idle? What is it that gentlemen wish? What would they have? Is life so dear, or peace so sweet, as to be purchased at the price of chains and slavery? Forbid it, Almighty God! I know not what course others may take; but as for me, give me liberty or give me death!

Boston Massacre Oration

By Joseph Warren

Boston. March 5th, 1772

Concerning Liberty and power.

When we turn over the historic page, and trace the rise and fall of states and empires, the mighty revolutions which have so often varied the face of the world strike our minds and with solemn surprise, and we are naturally led to endeavour to search out the causes of such astonishing changes.

That man is formed for social life, is an observation which, upon our first inquiry, presents itself immediately to our view, and our reason approves that wise and generous principle which actuated the first founders of civil government; an institution which hath its origin in the weakness of individuals, and hath for its end, the strength and security of all; and so long as the means of effecting this important end are thoroughly known, and religiously attended to, government is one of the richest blessings to mankind, and ought to be held in the highest veneration.

In young and new formed communities, the grand design of this institution is most generally understood, and most strictly regarded; the motives which urged to the social compact, cannot be at once forgotten, and that equality which is remembered to have subsisted so lately among them, prevents those who are clothed with authority from attempting to invade the freedom of their brethern; or if such an attempt is made, it prevents the community from suffering the offender to go unpunished; every member feels it to be his interest, and knows it to be his duty, to preserve inviolate the constitution on which the public safely depends.

It was this noble attachment to a free constitution, which raised ancient Rome from the smallest beginnings, to that bright summit of happiness and glory to which she arrived; and it was the loss of this which plunged her from that summit, into the black gulf of infamy and slavery. It was this attachment which inspired her senators with wisdom; it was this which glowed in the breasts of her heroes; it was this which guarded her liberties, and extended her dominions, gave peace at home, and commanded, respect abroad; and when this degenerated into tyrants and oppressors; her senators forgetful of their dignity, and seduced by base corruption, betrayed their country; her soldiers, regardless of their relation to the community, and urged only by hopes of plunder and rapine, unfeelingly committed the most flagrant enormities; and hired to the trade of death, with relentless fury they perpetrated the most cruel murders, whereby the streets of imperial Rome were drenched with her noblest blood. Thus this empress of the world lost her dominions abroad, and her inhabitants, dissolute in their manners, at length became contented slaves; and she stands to this day, the scorn and derision of nations, and a monument of this eternal truth, that public happiness depends on a virtuous and unshaken attachment to a free constitution.

It was this attachment to a constitution, founded on free and benevolent principles, which inspired the first settlers of this country: they saw with grief the daring outrages committed on the free constitution of their native land; they knew that nothing but a civil war could at that time restore its pristine purity. So hard was it to resolve to embrue their hands in the blood of their brethern, that they choose rather to quit their fair possessions, and seek another habitation in a distant clime. When they came to this new world, which they fairly purchased of the Indian natives, the only rightful proprietors, they cultivated the then barren soil, by their incessant labour, and defended their dear bought possessions with the fortitude of the Christian, and the bravery of the hero.

After various struggles, which, during the tyrannic reigns of the House of Stuart, were constantly kept up between right and wrong, between liberty and slavery, the connection between Great Britain and this colony, was settled in the reign of King William and Queen Mary, by a compact, the conditions of which were expressed in a charter; by which all the liberties and immunities of British subjects, were confined to this province, as fully and as absolutely as they possibly could be by any human instrument which can be devised. And it is undeniably true, that the greatest and most important right of a British subject is, that he shall be governed by no laws but those to which he either in person or by his representative hath given his consent: and this I will venture to assert is the grand basis of British freedom; it is interwoven with the constitution; and whenever this is lost, the constitution must be destroyed.

The British constitution (of which ours is a copy) is a happy compound of the three forms (under some of which all governments may be ranged) viz., monarchy, aristocracy, and democracy: of these three the British Legislature is composed, and without the consent of each branch, nothing can carry with it the force of a law; but when a law is to be passed for raising a tax, that law can originate only in the democratic branch, which is the House of Commons in Britain, and the House of Representatives here. The reason is obvious: they and their constituents are to pay much the largest part of it; but as the aristocratic branch, which is in Britain, the house of lords, and in this province, the council, are also to pay some part, their consent is necessary; and as the monarchic branch, which in Britain is the king, and with us, either the king in person, or the governor whom he shall be pleased to appoint to act in his stead, is supposed to have a just sense of his own interest, which is that of all the subjects in general. HIS consent is also necessary;

and when the consent of these three branches is obtained, the taxation is most certainly legal.

Let us now allow ourselves a few moments to examine the late acts of the British Parliament for taxing America. Let us with candour judge whether they are constitutionally binding upon us: if they are, in the name of justice let us submit to them, without murmuring one word.

First, I would ask whether the members of the British House of Commons are the democracy of this province? If they are, they are either the people of this province, or are elected by the people of this province, to represent them, and have therefore a constitutional right to originate a bill for taxing them: it is most certain they are neither; and therefore nothing done can be said to be done by the democratic branch of our constitution. I would next ask whether the Lords who compose the aristocratic branch of the legislature, are peers of America? I never heard it was (even in these extraordinary times) so much as pretended; and if they are not, certainly no act of theirs can be said to be the act of the aristocratic branch of our constitution. The power of the monarchic branch we with pleasure acknowledge, resides in the king, who may act either in person or by his representative; and I freely confess that I can see no reason why a proclamation for raising money in America, issued by the king's sole authority, would not be equally consistent with our own constitution, and therefore equally binding upon us with the late acts of the British Parliament for taxing us; for it is plain, that if there is any validity in those acts, it must arise altogether from the monarchical branch of the legislature: and I further think that it would be at least as equitable; for I do not conceive it to be of the least importance to us by whom our property is taken without our consent; and I am very much at loss to know by what figure of rhetoric, the inhabitants of this province can be called free subjects, when they are obliged to obey implicitly such laws as are made for them by men three thousand miles off, whom they know not, and whom they never have empowered to act for them; or how they can be said to have property when a body of men, over whom they have not the least control, and who are not in any way accountable to them, shall oblige them to deliver up any part, or the whole of their substance, without even asking their consent: and yet, whoever pretends that the late acts of the British Parliament for taxing America ought to be deemed binding upon us, must admit at once that we are absolute slaves, and have no property of our own; or else that we may be freemen, and at the same time under necessity of obeying the arbitrary commands of those over whom we have no control or influence; and that we have property of our own, which is entirely at the disposal of another. Such gross absurdities, I believe, will not be relished in this enlightened age: and it can be no matter of wonder that the people quickly perceived, and seriously complained of the inroads which these acts must unavoidably make upon their liberty, and of the hazard to which their whole property is by them exposed; for, if they may be taxed without their consent, even in the smallest trifle, they may also, without their consent, be deprived of every thing they possess, although never so valuable, never so dear. Certainly it never entered the hearts of our ancestors, that after so many dangers in this then desolate wilderness, their hard earned property should be at the disposal of the British Parliament; and as it was soon found that this taxation could not be supported by reason and argument, it seemed necessary that one act of oppression should be enforced by another, and therefore, contrary to our just rights as possessing, or at least having a just title to possess, all the liberties and immunities of British subjects, a standing army was established among us in a time of peace; and evidently for the purpose of effecting that, which it was one principal design of the founders of the constitution to prevent (when they declared a standing army in a time of peace to be against law) namely for the enforcement of obedience to acts which, upon fair examination, appeared to be unjust and unconstitutional.

The ruinous consequences of standing armies to free communities, may be seen in the histories of SYRACUSE, ROME, and many other once flourishing states; some of which have now scarce a name! Their baneful influence is most suddenly felt, when they are placed in populous cities; for by a corruption of morals, the public happiness is immediately affected? and that this is one of the effects of quartering troops in a populous city, is a truth, to which many a mourning parent, many a lost, despairing child in this metropolis must bear a very melancholy testimony. Soldiers are also taught to consider arms as the only arbiters by which every dispute is to be decided between contending states; they are instructed implicitly to obey their commanders, without inquiring into the justice of the cause they are engaged to support: hence it is, that they are ever to be dreaded as the ready engines of tyranny and oppression. And it is too observable that they are prone to introduce the same mode of decision in the disputes of individuals, and from thence have often arisen great animosities between them and the inhabitants, who, whilst in a naked defenceless state, are frequently insulted and abused by an armed soldiery. And this will be more especially the case, when the troops are informed that the intention of their being stationed in any city, is to overawe the inhabitants. That this was the avowed design of stationing an armed force in this town, is sufficiently known; and we, my fellow-citizens, have seen, we have felt the tragical effects! the fatal fifth of March, 1770, can never be forgotten. The horrors of that dreadful night are but too deeply impressed on our hearts. Language is too feeble to paint the emotions of our souls, when our streets were stained with the blood of our brethern; when our ears were wounded by the groans of the dying, and our eyes were tormented with the sight of the mangled bodies of the dead. When our alarmed imagination presented to our view our houses wrapt in flames, our children subjected to the barbarous caprice of the raging soldiery; our beauteous virgins exposed to all the insolence of unbridled passion; our virtuous wives, endeared to us by every tender tie, falling a sacrifice to worse than brutal violence, and perhaps, like the famed Lucretia, distracted with anguish and despair, ending their wretched lives by their own fair hands. When we beheld the authors of our distress parading in our streets or drawn up in a regular battalia, as though in a hostile city, our hearts beat to arms; we snatched our weapons, almost resolved, by one decisive stroke, to avenge the death of our slaughtered brethern, and to secure from future danger, all that we held most dear: but propitious Heaven forbad the bloody carnage, and saved the threatened victims of our keen resentment, not by their discipline, not by their regular army; no, it was royal George's livery that provided their shield, it was that which turned the pointed engines of destruction from their breasts(2). The thoughts of vengeance were soon buried in our inbred affection to Great Britain, and calm reason dictated a method of removing the troops more mild than an immediate recourse to the sword. With united efforts you urged the immediate departure of the troops from the town; you urged it, with a resolution which ensured success; you obtained your wishes, and the removal of the troops was effected, without one drop of their blood being shed by the inhabitants.

The immediate actors in the tragedy of trhat night were surrendered to justice. It is not mine to say how far they were guilty! They have been tried by the country and acquitted of murder! and they are not to be again arraigned at an earthly bar: but surely the men who have promiscuously scattered death amidst the innocent inhabitants of a popular city, ought to see well to it that they be prepared to stand at the bar of an omniscient Judge! and all who contrived or encouraged the stationing of troops in this place, have reasons of eternal importance, to reflect with deep contrition, on their base designs, and humbly to repent of their impious machinations.

The infatuation which hath seemed, for a number of years, to prevail in the British councils, with regard to us, is truly astonishing! what can be proposed by the our freedom, I really cannot surmise; even leaving justice and humanity out of the question, I do not know one single advantage which can arise to the British nation, from our being enslaved; I know not of any gains, which can be wrung from us by oppression, which they may not obtain from us by our own consent, in the smooth channel of commerce; we wish the wealth and prosperity of Britain; we contribute largely to both. Doth what we contribute lose all its value, because it is done voluntarily? The amazing increase of riches to Britain, the great rise of the value of her lands, the flourishing state of her navy are striking proofs of the advantages derived to her from her commerce with the colonies; and it is our earnest desire that she may still continue to enjoy the same emoluments, until her streets are paved with American gold; only, let us have the pleasure of calling it our own, whilst it is in our hands; but this it seems is too great a favour: we are to be governed by the absolute commands of others; our property is to be taken away without our consent; if we complain, our complaints are treated with contempt; if we assert our rights, that assertion is deemed insolence; if we humbly offer to submit the matter to the imperial decision of reason, the sword is judged the most proper argument to silence our murmurs! but this cannot be the case: surely the British nation will not suffer the reputation of their justice and their honour, to be thus sported away by a capricious ministry; no, they will in a short time open their eyes to their true interest: they nourish in their own breasts, a noble love of liberty; they hold her dear, and they know that all who have once possessed her charms, had rather die than suffer her to be torn from their embraces; they are also sensible that Britain is so deeply interested in the prosperity of the colonies, that she must eventually feel every wound given to their freedom; they cannot be ignorant that more dependence may be placed on the affections of a brother, than on the forced service of a slave; they must approve your efforts for the preservation of your rights; from a sympathy of soul they must pray for your success;

and I doubt not but they will, ere long, exert themselves effectually, to redress your grievances. Even in the dissolute reign of King Charles II when the House of Commons impeached the Earl of Clarendon of high treason, the first article on which they founded their accusation was, that "he had designed a standing army to be raised, and to govern the kingdom thereby." And the eighth article was, that "he had introduced an arbitrary government into his majesty's plantation." A terrifying example to those who are now forging chains for this country.

You have, my friends and countrymen, frustrated the designs of your enemies, by your unanimity and fortitude: it was your union and determined spirit which expelled those troops who polluted your streets with innocent blood. You have appointed this anniversary as a standing memorial of the bloody consequences of placing an armed force in a populous city, and of your deliverance from the dangers which then seemed to hang over your heads: and I am confident that you never will betray the least want of spirit when called upon to guard your freedom. None but they who set a just value upon the blessings of liberty are worthy to enjoy her; your illustrious fathers were her zealous votaries; when the blasting frowns of tyranny drove her from public view, they clasped her in their arms, they cherished her in their generous bosoms, they brought her safe over the rough ocean, and fixed her seat in this then dreary wilderness; they nursed her infant age with the most tender care; for her sake, they patiently bore the severest hardships; for her support, they underwent the most rugged toils: in her defence, they boldly encountered the most alarming dangers; neither the ravenous beasts that ranged the woods for prey, nor the more furious savages of the wilderness, could damp their ardour! Whilst with one hand they broke the stubborn glebe, with the other they grasped their weapons, ever ready to protect her from danger. No sacrifice, not even their own blood, was esteemed too rich a libation for her altar! God prospered their valour; they preserved her brillancy unsullied; they enjoyed her whilst they lived, and dying, bequeathed the dear inheritance to your care. And as they left you this glorious legacy, they have undoubtedly transmitted to you some portion of their noble spirit, to inspire you with virtue to merit her, and courage to preserve her: you surely cannot, with such examples before our eyes, as every page of the history of this country affords(3), suffer your liberties to be ravished from you by lawless force, or cajoled away by flattery and fraud.

The voice of your fathers' blood cries to you from the ground; MY SONS SCORN TO BE SLAVES! in vain we met the frowns of tyrants; in vain, we crossed the boisterous ocean, found a new world, and prepared it for the happy residence of liberty; in vain, we toiled; in vain, we fought; we bled in vain, if you, our offspring, want valour to repel the assaults of her invaders! Stain not the glory of your worthy ancestors; but like them resolve, never to part with your birthright; be wise in your deliberations, and determined in your exertions for the preservation of your liberties. Follow not the dictates of passion, but enlist yourselves under the sacred banner of reason; use every method in your power to secure your rights; at least prevent the curses of posterity from being heaped upon your memories.

If you, with united zeal and fortitude, oppose the torrent of oppression; if you feel the true fire of patriotism burning in your breasts; if you, from your souls, despise the most gaudy dress that slavery can wear; if you really prefer the lonely cottage (whilst blest with liberty) to gilded palaces, surrounded with the ensigns of slavery, you may have the fullest assurance that tyranny, with her accursed train, will hide their hideous heads in confusion, shame and despair; if you perform your part, you must have the strongest confidence that THE SAME ALMIGHTY BEING who protected your pious and venerable forefathers, who enabled them to turn a barren wilderness into a fruitful field, who so often made bare his arms for their salvation, will still be mindful of you their offspring.

May THIS ALMIGHTY BEING graciously preside in all our councils. May he direct us to such measures as he himself shall approve, and be pleased to bless. May we ever be a people. favoured of GOD. May our land be a land of liberty, the seat of virtue, the asylum of the oppressed, a name and a praise in the whole earth, until the last shock of time shall bury the empires of the world in one common undistinguished ruin!

WOODROW POLSTON

Patrick Henry Speech in the Virginia Convention

16 June 1788

Mr. Chairman.—*The necessity of a Bill of Rights appear(s) to me to be greater in this Government, than ever it was in any Government before. I observed already, that the sense of the European nations, and particularly Great-Britain, is against the construction of rights being retained, which are not expressly relinquished. I repeat, that all nations have adopted this construction—That all rights not expressly and unequivocally reserved to the people, are impliedly and incidentally relinquished to rulers; as necessarily inseparable from the delegated powers. It is so in Great-Britain: For every possible right which is not reserved to the people by some express provision or compact, is within the King's prerogative. It is so in that country which is said to be in such full possession of freedom. It is so in Spain, Germany, and other parts of the world. Let us consider the sentiments which have been entertained by the people of America on this subject. At the revolution, it must be admitted, that it was their sense to put down those great rights which ought in all countries to be held inviolable and sacred. Virginia did so we all remember. She made a compact to reserve, expressly, certain rights. When fortified with full, adequate, and abundant representation, was she satisfied with that representation? No.—She most cautiously and guardedly reserved and secured those invaluable, inestimable rights and privileges, which no people, inspired with the least glow of the patriotic love of liberty, ever did, or ever can, abandon. She is called upon now to abandon them, and dissolve that compact which secured them to her. She is called upon to accede to another compact which most infallibly supercedes and annihilates her present one. Will she do it?—This is the question. If you intend to reserve your unalienable rights, you must have the most express stipulation. For if implication be allowed, you are ousted of those rights. If the people do not think it necessary to reserve them, they will be supposed to be given up. How were the Congressional rights defined when the people of America united by a confederacy to defend their liberties and rights against the tyrannical attempts of Great-Britain? The States were not then contented with implied reservation. No, Mr. Chairman. It was expressly declared in our Confederation that every right was retained by the States respectively, which was not given up to the Government of the United States. But there is no such thing here. You therefore by a natural and unavoidable implication, give up your rights to the General Government. Your own example furnishes an argument against it. If you give up these powers, without a Bill of Rights, you will exhibit the most absurd thing to mankind that ever the world saw—A Government that has abandoned all its powers—The powers of (a) direct taxation, the sword, and the purse. You have disposed of them to Congress, without a Bill of Rights—without check, limitation, or controul. And still you have checks and guards— still you keep barriers—pointed where? Pointed against your weakened, prostrated, enervated State Government! You have a Bill of Rights to defend you against the State Government, which is bereaved of all power; and yet you have none against Congress, though in full and exclusive possession of all power! You arm yourselves against the weak and defenceless, and expose yourselves naked to the armed and powerful. Is not this a conduct of unexampled absurdity? What barriers have you to oppose to this most strong energetic Government? To that Government you have nothing to oppose. All your defence is given up. This is a real actual defect.—It must strike the mind of every Gentleman. When our Government was first instituted in Virginia, we declared the common law of England to be in force.—That system of law which has been admired, and has protected 2 us and our ancestors, is excluded by that system.—Added to this, we adopted a Bill of Rights. By this Constitution, some of the best barriers of human rights are thrown away. Is there not an additional reason to have a Bill of Rights? By the ancient common law, the trial of all facts is decided by a jury of impartial men from the immediate vicinage. This paper speaks of different juries from the common law, in criminal cases; and in civil controversies excludes trial by jury altogether. There is therefore more occasion for the supplementary check of a Bill of Rights now, than then. Congress from their general powers may fully go into the business of human legislation. They may legislate in criminal cases from treason to the lowest offence, petty larceny. They may define crimes and prescribe punishments. In the definition of crimes, I trust they will be directed by what wise Representatives ought to be governed by. But when we come to punishments, no latitude ought to be left, nor dependence put on the virtue of Representatives. What says our Bill of Rights? "That excessive bail ought not to be required, nor excessive fines imposed, nor cruel and unusual punishments inflicted." Are you not therefore now calling on those Gentlemen who are to compose Congress, to prescribe trials and define punishments without this controul? Will they find sentiments there similar to this Bill of Rights? You let them loose—you do more—you depart from the genius of your country. That paper tells you, that the trial of crimes shall be by jury, and held in the State where the crime shall have been committed.—Under this extensive provision, they may proceed in a manner extremely dangerous to liberty.—Persons accused may be carried from one extremity of the State to another, and be tried not by an impartial jury of the vicinage, acquainted with his character, and the circumstances of the fact; but by a jury unacquainted with both, and who may be biassed against him.—Is not this sufficient to alarm men?— How different is this from the immemor[i]al practice of your British ancestors, and your own? I need not tell you, that by the common law a number of hundredors were required to be on a jury, and that afterwards it was sufficient if the jurors came from the same county. With less than this the people of England have never been satisfied. That paper ought to have declared the common law in force. In this business of legislation, your Members of Congress will lose the restriction of not imposing excessive fines, demanding excessive bail, and inflicting cruel and unusual punishments.—These are prohibited by your Declaration of Rights. What has distinguished our ancestors?—That they would not admit of tortures, or cruel and barbarous punishments. But Congress may introduce the practice of the civil law, in preference to that of the common law.—They may introduce the practice of France, Spain, and Germany—Of torturing to extort a confession of the crime. They will say that they might as well draw examples from those countries as from Great-Britain; and they will tell you, that there is such a necessity of strengthening the arm of Government, that they must have a criminal equity, and extort confession by torture, in order to punish with still more relentless severity. We are then lost and undone.—And can any man think it troublesome, when we can by a small interference prevent our rights from being lost?—If you will, like the Virginian Government, give them knowledge of the extent of the rights retained by the people, and the powers themselves, they will, if they be honest men, thank you for it.—Will they not wish to go on sure grounds?—But if you leave them otherwise, they will not know how to proceed; and being in a state of uncertainty, they will assume rather than give up powers by implication. A Bill of Rights may be 3 summed up in a few words. What do they tell us?—That our rights are reserved.—Why not say so? Is it because it will consume too much paper? Gentlemen's reasonings against a Bill of Rights, do not satisfy me. Without saying which has the right side, it remains doubtful. A Bill of Rights is a favourite thing with the Virginians, and the people of the other States likewise. It may be their prejudice, but the Government ought to suit their geniuses, otherwise its operation will be unhappy. A Bill of Rights, even if its necessity be doubtful, will exclude the possibility of dispute, and with great submission, I think the best way is to have no dispute. In the present Constitution, they are restrained from issuing general warrants to search suspected places, or seize persons not named, without evidence of the commission of a fact, &c. There was certainly some celestial influence governing those who deliberated on that Constitution:— For they have with the most cautious and enlightened circumspection, guarded those indefeasible rights, which ought ever to be* held sacred. The officers of Congress may come upon you, fortified with all the terrors of paramount federal authority.—Excisemen may come in multitudes:—For the limitation of their numbers no man knows.—They may, unless the General Government be restrained by a Bill of Rights, or some similar restriction, go into your cellars and rooms, and search, ransack and measure, every thing you eat, drink and wear. They ought to be restrained within proper bounds. With respect to the freedom of the press, I need say nothing; for it is hoped that the Gentlemen who shall compose Congress, will take care as little as possible, to infringe the rights of human nature.—This will result from their integrity. They should from prudence, abstain from violating the rights of their constituents. They are not however expressly restrained.—But whether they will intermeddle with that palladium of our liberties or not, I leave you to determine.

First Inaugural Address

George Washington

Fellow-Citizens of the Senate and of the House of Representatives:
Among the vicissitudes incident to life no event could have filled me with greater anxieties than that of which the notification was transmitted by your order, and received on the 14th day of the present month. On the one hand, I was summoned by my Country, whose voice I can never hear but with veneration and love, from a retreat which I had chosen with the fondest predilection, and, in my flattering hopes, with an immutable decision, as the asylum of my declining years--a retreat which was rendered every day more necessary as well as more dear to me by the addition of habit to inclination, and of frequent interruptions in my health to the gradual waste committed on it by time. On the other hand, the magnitude and difficulty of the trust to which the voice of my country called me, being sufficient to awaken in the wisest and most experienced of her citizens a distrustful scrutiny into his qualifications, could not but overwhelm with despondence one who (inheriting inferior endowments from nature and unpracticed in the duties of civil administration) ought to be peculiarly conscious of his own deficiencies. In this conflict of emotions all I dare aver is that it has been my

faithful study to collect my duty from a just appreciation of every circumstance by which it might be affected. All I dare hope is that if, in executing this task, I have been too much swayed by a grateful remembrance of former instances, or by an affectionate sensibility to this transcendent proof of the confidence of my fellow-citizens, and have thence too little consulted my incapacity as well as disinclination for the weighty and untried cares before me, my error will be palliated by the motives which mislead me, and its consequences be judged by my country with some share of the partiality in which they originated.

Such being the impressions under which I have, in obedience to the public summons, repaired to the present station, it would be peculiarly improper to omit in this first official act my fervent supplications to that Almighty Being who rules over the universe, who presides in the councils of nations, and whose providential aids can supply every human defect, that His benediction may consecrate to the liberties and happiness of the people of the United States a Government instituted by themselves for these essential purposes, and may enable every instrument employed in its administration to execute with success the functions allotted to his charge. In tendering this homage to the Great Author of every public and private good, I assure myself that it expresses your sentiments not less than my own, nor those of my fellow- citizens at large less than either. No people can be bound to acknowledge and adore the Invisible Hand which conducts the affairs of men more than those of the United States. Every step by which they have advanced to the character of an independent nation seems to have been distinguished by some token of providential agency; and in the important revolution just accomplished in the system of their united government the tranquil deliberations and voluntary consent of so many distinct communities from which the event has resulted can not be compared with the means by which most governments have been established without some return of pious gratitude, along with an humble anticipation of the future blessings which the past seem to presage. These reflections, arising out of the present crisis, have forced themselves too strongly on my mind to be suppressed. You will join with me, I trust, in thinking that there are none under the influence of which the proceedings of a new and free government can more auspiciously commence.

By the article establishing the executive department, it is made the duty of the President "to recommend to your consideration such measures as he shall judge necessary and expedient." The circumstances under which I now meet you will acquit me from entering into that subject further than to refer to the great constitutional charter under which you are assembled, and which, in defining your powers, designates the objects to which your attention is to be given. It will be more consistent with those circumstances, and far more congenial with the feelings which actuate me, to substitute, in place of a recommendation of particular measures, the tribute that is due to the talents, the rectitude, and the patriotism which adorn the characters selected to devise and adopt them. In these honorable qualifications I behold the surest pledges that as on one side no local prejudices or attachments, no separate views nor party animosities, will misdirect the comprehensive and equal eye which ought to watch over this great assemblage of communities and interests, so, on another, that the foundation of our national policy will be laid in the pure and immutable principles of private morality, and the preeminence of free government be exemplified by all the attributes which can win the affections of its citizens and command the respect of the world. I dwell on this prospect with every satisfaction which an ardent love for my country can inspire, since there is no truth more thoroughly established than that there exists in the economy and course of nature an indissoluble union between virtue and happiness; between duty and advantage; between the genuine maxims of an honest and magnanimous policy and the solid rewards of public prosperity and felicity; since we ought to be no less persuaded that the propitious smiles of Heaven can never be expected on a nation that disregards the eternal rules of order and right which Heaven itself has ordained; and since the preservation of the sacred fire of liberty and the destiny of the republican model of government are justly considered, perhaps, as deeply, as finally, staked on the experiment entrusted to the hands of the American people.

Besides the ordinary objects submitted to your care, it will remain with your judgment to decide how far an exercise of the occasional power delegated by the fifth article of the Constitution is rendered expedient at the present juncture by the nature of objections which have been urged against the system, or by the degree of inquietude which has given birth to them. Instead of undertaking particular recommendations on this subject, in which I could be guided by no lights derived from official opportunities, I shall again give way to my entire confidence in your discernment and pursuit of the public good; for I assure myself that whilst you carefully avoid every alteration which might endanger the benefits of an united and effective government, or which ought to await the future lessons of experience, a reverence for the characteristic rights of freemen and a regard for the public harmony will sufficiently influence your deliberations on the question how far the former can be impregnably fortified or the latter be safely and advantageously promoted.

To the foregoing observations I have one to add, which will be most properly addressed to the House of Representatives. It concerns myself, and will therefore be as brief as possible. When I was first honored with a call into the service of my country, then on the eve of an arduous struggle for its liberties, the light in which I contemplated my duty required that I should renounce every pecuniary compensation. From this resolution I have in no instance departed; and being still under the impressions which produced it, I must decline as inapplicable to myself any share in the personal emoluments which may be indispensably included in a permanent provision for the executive department, and must accordingly pray that the pecuniary estimates for the station in which I am placed may during my continuance in it be limited to such actual expenditures as the public good may be thought to require.

Having thus imparted to you my sentiments as they have been awakened by the occasion which brings us together, I shall take my present leave; but not without resorting once more to the benign Parent of the Human Race in humble supplication that, since He has been pleased to favor the American people with opportunities for deliberating in perfect tranquillity, and dispositions for deciding with unparalleled unanimity on a form of government for the security of their union and the advancement of their happiness, so His divine blessing may be equally conspicuous in the enlarged views, the temperate consultations, and the wise measures on which the success of this Government must depend.

Farewell Address
George Washington

Friends and Citizens:
The period for a new election of a citizen to administer the executive government of the United States being not far distant, and the time actually arrived when your thoughts must be employed in designating the person who is to be clothed with that important trust, it appears to me proper, especially as it may conduce to a more distinct expression of the public voice, that I should now apprise you of the resolution I have formed, to decline being considered among the number of those out of whom a choice is to be made.

I beg you, at the same time, to do me the justice to be assured that this resolution has not been taken without a strict regard to all the considerations appertaining to the relation which binds a dutiful citizen to his country; and that in withdrawing the tender of service, which silence in my situation might imply, I am influenced by no diminution of zeal for your future interest, no deficiency of grateful respect for your past kindness, but am supported by a full conviction that the step is compatible with both.

The acceptance of, and continuance hitherto in, the office to which your suffrages have twice called me have been a uniform sacrifice of inclination to the opinion of duty and to a deference for what appeared to be your desire. I constantly hoped that it would have been much earlier in my power, consistently with motives which I was not at liberty to disregard, to return to that retirement from which I had been reluctantly drawn. The strength of my inclination to do this, previous to the last election, had even led to the preparation of an address to declare it to you; but mature reflection on the then perplexed and critical posture of our affairs with foreign nations, and the unanimous advice of persons entitled to my confidence, impelled me to abandon the idea.

I rejoice that the state of your concerns, external as well as internal, no longer renders the pursuit of inclination incompatible with the sentiment of duty or propriety, and am persuaded, whatever partiality may be retained for my services, that, in the present circumstances of our country, you will not disapprove my determination to retire.

The impressions with which I first undertook the arduous trust were explained on the proper occasion. In the discharge of this trust, I will only say that I have, with good intentions, contributed towards the organization and administration of the government the best exertions of which a very fallible judgment was capable. Not unconscious in the outset of the inferiority of my qualifications, experience in my own eyes, perhaps still more in the eyes of others, has strengthened the motives to diffidence of myself; and every day the increasing weight of years admonishes me more and more that the shade of retirement is as necessary to me as it will be welcome. Satisfied that if any circumstances have given peculiar value to my services, they were temporary, I have the consolation to believe that, while choice and prudence invite me to quit the political scene, patriotism does not forbid it.

In looking forward to the moment which is intended to terminate the career of my public life, my feelings do not permit me to suspend the deep acknowledgment of that debt of gratitude which I owe to my beloved country for the many honors it has conferred upon me; still more for the steadfast confidence with which it has supported me; and for the opportunities I have thence enjoyed of manifesting my inviolable attachment, by services faithful and persevering, though in usefulness unequal to my zeal. If benefits have resulted to our country from these services, let it always be remembered to your praise, and as an instructive example in our annals, that under circumstances in which the passions, agitated in every direction, were liable to mislead, amidst appearances sometimes dubious, vicissitudes of fortune often discouraging, in situations in which not unfrequently want of success has countenanced the spirit of criticism, the constancy of your support was the essential prop of the efforts, and a guarantee of the plans by which they were effected. Profoundly penetrated with this idea, I shall carry it with me to my grave, as a strong incitement to unceasing vows that heaven may continue to you the choicest tokens of its beneficence; that your union and brotherly affection may be perpetual; that the free Constitution, which is the work of your hands, may be sacredly maintained; that its administration in every department may be stamped with wisdom and virtue; that, in fine, the happiness of the people of these States, under the auspices of liberty, may be made complete by so careful a preservation and so prudent a use of this blessing as will acquire to them the glory of recommending it to the applause, the affection, and adoption of every nation which is yet a stranger to it.

Here, perhaps, I ought to stop. But a solicitude for your welfare, which cannot end but with my life, and the apprehension of danger, natural to that solicitude, urge me, on an occasion like the present, to offer to your solemn contemplation, and to recommend to your frequent review, some sentiments which are the result of much reflection, of no inconsiderable observation, and which appear to me all-important to the permanency of your felicity as a people. These will be offered to you with the more freedom, as you can only see in them the disinterested warnings of a parting friend, who can possibly have no personal motive to bias his counsel. Nor can I forget, as an encouragement to it, your indulgent reception of my sentiments on a former and not dissimilar occasion.

Interwoven as is the love of liberty with every ligament of your hearts, no recommendation of mine is necessary to fortify or confirm the attachment.

The unity of government which constitutes you one people is also now dear to you. It is justly so, for it is a main pillar in the edifice of your real independence, the support of your tranquility at home, your peace abroad; of your safety; of your prosperity; of that very liberty which you so highly prize. But as it is easy to foresee that, from different causes and from different quarters, much pains will be taken, many artifices employed to weaken in your minds the conviction of this truth; as this is the point in your political fortress against which the batteries of internal and external enemies will be most constantly and actively (though often covertly and insidiously) directed, it is of infinite moment that you should properly estimate the immense value of your national union to your collective and individual happiness; that you should cherish a cordial, habitual, and immovable attachment to it; accustoming yourselves to think and speak of it as of the palladium of your political safety and prosperity; watching for its preservation with jealous anxiety; discountenancing whatever may suggest even a suspicion that it can in any event be abandoned; and indignantly frowning upon the first dawning of every attempt to alienate any portion of our country from the rest, or to enfeeble the sacred ties which now link together the various parts.

For this you have every inducement of sympathy and interest. Citizens, by birth or choice, of a common country, that country has a right to concentrate your affections. The name of American, which belongs to you in your national capacity, must always exalt the just pride of patriotism more than any appellation derived from local discriminations. With slight shades of difference, you have the same religion, manners, habits, and political principles. You have in a common cause fought and triumphed together; the independence and liberty you possess are the work of joint counsels, and joint efforts of common dangers, sufferings, and successes.

But these considerations, however powerfully they address themselves to your sensibility, are greatly outweighed by those which apply more immediately to your interest. Here every portion of our country finds the most commanding motives for carefully guarding and preserving the union of the whole.

The North, in an unrestrained intercourse with the South, protected by the equal laws of a common government, finds in the productions of the latter great additional resources of maritime and commercial enterprise and precious materials of manufacturing industry. The South, in the same intercourse, benefiting by the agency of the North, sees its agriculture grow and its commerce expand. Turning partly into its own channels the seamen of the North, it finds its particular navigation invigorated; and, while it contributes, in different ways, to nourish and increase the general mass of the national navigation, it looks forward to the protection of a maritime strength, to which itself is unequally adapted. The East, in a like intercourse with the West, already finds, and in the progressive improvement of interior communications by land and water, will more and more find a valuable vent for the commodities which it brings from abroad, or manufactures at home. The West derives from the East supplies requisite to its growth and comfort, and, what is perhaps of still greater consequence, it must of necessity owe the secure enjoyment of indispensable outlets for its own productions to the weight, influence, and the future maritime strength of the Atlantic side of the Union, directed by an indissoluble community of interest as one nation. Any other tenure by which the West can hold this essential advantage, whether derived from its own separate strength, or from an apostate and unnatural connection with any foreign power, must be intrinsically precarious.

While, then, every part of our country thus feels an immediate and particular interest in union, all the parts combined cannot fail to find in the united mass of means and efforts greater strength, greater resource, proportionably greater security from external danger, a less frequent interruption of their peace by foreign nations; and, what is of inestimable value, they must derive from union an exemption from those broils and wars between themselves, which so frequently afflict neighboring countries not tied together by the same governments, which their own rival ships alone would be sufficient to produce, but which opposite foreign alliances, attachments, and intrigues would stimulate and embitter. Hence, likewise, they will avoid the necessity of those overgrown military establishments which, under any form of government, are inauspicious to liberty, and which are to be regarded as particularly hostile to republican liberty. In this sense it is that your union ought to be considered as a main prop of your liberty, and that the love of the one ought to endear to you the preservation of the other.

These considerations speak a persuasive language to every reflecting and virtuous mind, and exhibit the continuance of the Union as a primary object of patriotic desire. Is there a doubt whether a common government can embrace so large a sphere? Let experience solve it. To listen to mere speculation in such a case were criminal. We are authorized to hope that a proper organization of the whole with the auxiliary agency of governments for the respective subdivisions, will afford a happy issue to the experiment. It is well worth a fair and full experiment. With such powerful and obvious motives to union, affecting all parts of our country, while experience shall not have demonstrated its impracticability, there will always be reason to distrust the patriotism of those who in any quarter may endeavor to weaken its bands.

In contemplating the causes which may disturb our Union, it occurs as matter of serious concern that any ground should have been furnished for characterizing parties by geographical discriminations, Northern and Southern, Atlantic and Western; whence designing men may endeavor to excite a belief that there is a real difference of local interests and views. One of the expedients of party to acquire influence within particular districts is to misrepresent the opinions and aims of other districts. You cannot shield yourselves too much against the jealousies and heartburnings which spring from these misrepresentations; they tend to render alien to each other those who ought to be bound together by fraternal affection. The inhabitants of our Western country have lately had a useful lesson on this head; they have seen, in the negotiation by the Executive, and in the unanimous ratification by the Senate, of the treaty with Spain, and in the universal satisfaction at that event, throughout the United States, a decisive proof how unfounded were the suspicions propagated among them of a policy in the General Government and in the Atlantic States unfriendly to their interests in regard to the Mississippi; they have been witnesses to the formation of two treaties, that with Great Britain, and that with Spain, which secure to them everything they could desire, in respect to our foreign relations, towards confirming their prosperity. Will it not be their wisdom to rely for the preservation of these advantages on the Union by which they were procured ? Will they not henceforth be deaf to those advisers, if such there are, who would sever them from their brethren and connect them with aliens?

To the efficacy and permanency of your Union, a government for the whole is indispensable. No alliance, however strict, between the parts can be an adequate substitute; they must inevitably experience the infractions and interruptions which all alliances in all times have experienced. Sensible of this momentous truth, you have improved upon your first essay, by the adoption of a constitution of government better calculated than your former for an intimate union, and for the efficacious management of your common concerns. This government, the offspring of our own choice, uninfluenced and unawed, adopted upon full investigation and mature deliberation, completely free in its principles, in the distribution of its powers, uniting security with energy, and containing within itself a provision for its own amendment, has a just claim to your confidence and your support. Respect for its authority, compliance with its laws, acquiescence in its measures, are duties enjoined by the fundamental maxims of true liberty. The basis of our political systems is the right of the people to make and to alter their constitutions of government. But the Constitution which at any time exists, till changed by an explicit and authentic act of the whole people, is sacredly obligatory upon all. The very idea of the power and the right of the people to establish government presupposes the duty of every individual to obey the established government.

All obstructions to the execution of the laws, all combinations and associations, under whatever plausible character, with the real design to direct, control, counteract, or awe the regular deliberation and action of the constituted authorities, are destructive of this fundamental principle, and of fatal tendency. They serve to organize faction, to give it an artificial and extraordinary force; to put, in the place of the delegated will of the nation the will of a party, often a small but artful and enterprising minority of the community; and, according to the alternate triumphs of different parties, to make the public administration the mirror of the ill-concerted and incongruous projects of faction, rather than the organ of consistent and wholesome plans digested by common counsels and modified by mutual interests.

However combinations or associations of the above description may now and then answer popular ends, they are likely, in the course of time and things, to become potent engines, by which cunning, ambitious, and unprincipled men will be enabled to subvert the power of the people and to usurp for themselves the reins of government, destroying afterwards the very engines which have lifted them to unjust dominion.

Towards the preservation of your government, and the permanency of your present happy state, it is requisite, not only that you steadily discountenance

irregular oppositions to its acknowledged authority, but also that you resist with care the spirit of innovation upon its principles, however specious the pretexts. One method of assault may be to effect, in the forms of the Constitution, alterations which will impair the energy of the system, and thus to undermine what cannot be directly overthrown. In all the changes to which you may be invited, remember that time and habit are at least as necessary to fix the true character of governments as of other human institutions; that experience is the surest standard by which to test the real tendency of the existing constitution of a country; that facility in changes, upon the credit of mere hypothesis and opinion, exposes to perpetual change, from the endless variety of hypothesis and opinion; and remember, especially, that for the efficient management of your common interests, in a country so extensive as ours, a government of as much vigor as is consistent with the perfect security of liberty is indispensable. Liberty itself will find in such a government, with powers properly distributed and adjusted, its surest guardian. It is, indeed, little else than a name, where the government is too feeble to withstand the enterprises of faction, to confine each member of the society within the limits prescribed by the laws, and to maintain all in the secure and tranquil enjoyment of the rights of person and property.
I have already intimated to you the danger of parties in the State, with particular reference to the

founding of them on geographical discriminations. Let me now take a more comprehensive view, and warn you in the most solemn manner against the baneful effects of the spirit of party generally.

This spirit, unfortunately, is inseparable from our nature, having its root in the strongest passions of the human mind. It exists under different shapes in all governments, more or less stifled, controlled, or repressed; but, in those of the popular form, it is seen in its greatest rankness, and is truly their worst enemy.

The alternate domination of one faction over another, sharpened by the spirit of revenge, natural to party dissension, which in different ages and countries has perpetrated the most horrid enormities, is itself a frightful despotism. But this leads at length to a more formal and permanent despotism. The disorders and miseries which result gradually incline the minds of men to seek security and repose in the absolute power of an individual; and sooner or later the chief of some prevailing faction, more able or more fortunate than his competitors, turns this disposition to the purposes of his own elevation, on the ruins of public liberty.

Without looking forward to an extremity of this kind (which nevertheless ought not to be entirely out of sight), the common and continual mischiefs of the spirit of party are sufficient to make it the interest and duty of a wise people to discourage and restrain it.

It serves always to distract the public councils and enfeeble the public administration. It agitates the community with ill-founded jealousies and false alarms, kindles the animosity of one part against another, foments occasionally riot and insurrection. It opens the door to foreign influence and corruption, which finds a facilitated access to the government itself through the channels of party passions. Thus the policy and the will of one country are subjected to the policy and will of another.

There is an opinion that parties in free countries are useful checks upon the administration of the government and serve to keep alive the spirit of liberty. This within certain limits is probably true; and in governments of a monarchical cast, patriotism may look with indulgence, if not with favor, upon the spirit of party. But in those of the popular character, in governments purely elective, it is a spirit not to be encouraged. From their natural tendency, it is certain there will always be enough of that spirit for every salutary purpose. And there being constant danger of excess, the effort ought to be by force of public opinion, to mitigate and assuage it. A fire not to be quenched, it demands a uniform vigilance to prevent its bursting into a flame, lest, instead of warming, it should consume.

It is important, likewise, that the habits of thinking in a free country should inspire caution in those entrusted with its administration, to confine themselves within their respective constitutional spheres, avoiding in the exercise of the powers of one department to encroach upon another. The spirit of encroachment tends to consolidate the powers of all the departments in one, and thus to create, whatever the form of government, a real despotism. A just estimate of that love of power, and proneness to abuse it, which predominates in the human heart, is sufficient to satisfy us of the truth of this position. The necessity of reciprocal checks in the exercise of political power, by dividing and distributing it into different depositaries, and constituting each the guardian of the public weal against invasions by the others, has been evinced by experiments ancient and modern; some of them in our country and under our own eyes. To preserve them must be as necessary as to institute them. If, in the opinion of the people, the distribution or modification of the constitutional powers be in any particular wrong, let it be corrected by an amendment in the way which the constitution designates. But let there be no change by usurpation; for though this, in one instance, may be the instrument of good, it is the customary weapon by which free governments are destroyed. The precedent must always greatly overbalance in permanent evil any partial or transient benefit, which the use can at any time yield.

Of all the dispositions and habits which lead to political prosperity, religion and morality are indispensable supports. In vain would that man claim the tribute of patriotism, who should labor to subvert these great pillars of human happiness, these firmest props of the duties of men and citizens. The mere politician, equally with the pious man, ought to respect and to cherish them. A volume could not trace all their connections with private and public felicity. Let it simply be asked: Where is the security for property, for reputation, for life, if the sense of religious obligation desert the oaths which are the instruments of investigation in courts of justice? And let us with caution indulge the supposition that morality can be maintained without religion. Whatever may be conceded to the influence of refined education on minds of peculiar structure, reason and experience both forbid us to expect that national morality can prevail in exclusion of religious principle.

It is substantially true that virtue or morality is a necessary spring of popular government. The rule, indeed, extends with more or less force to every species of free government. Who that is a sincere friend to it can look with indifference upon attempts to shake the foundation of the fabric?

Promote then, as an object of primary importance, institutions for the general diffusion of knowledge. In proportion as the structure of a government gives force to public opinion, it is essential that public opinion should be enlightened.

As a very important source of strength and security, cherish public credit. One method of preserving it is to use it as sparingly as possible, avoiding occasions of expense by cultivating peace, but remembering also that timely disbursements to prepare for danger frequently prevent much greater disbursements to repel it, avoiding likewise the accumulation of debt, not only by shunning occasions of expense, but by vigorous exertion in time of peace to discharge the debts which unavoidable wars may have occasioned, not ungenerously throwing upon posterity the burden which we ourselves ought to bear. The execution of these maxims belongs to your representatives, but it is necessary that public opinion should co-operate. To facilitate to them the performance of their duty, it is essential that you should practically bear in mind that towards the payment of debts there must be revenue; that to have revenue there must be taxes; that no taxes can be devised which are not more or less inconvenient and unpleasant; that the intrinsic embarrassment, inseparable from the selection of the proper objects (which is always a choice of difficulties), ought to be a decisive motive for a candid construction of the conduct of the government in making it, and for a spirit of acquiescence in the measures for obtaining revenue, which the public exigencies may at any time dictate.

Observe good faith and justice towards all nations; cultivate peace and harmony with all. Religion and morality enjoin this conduct; and can it be, that good policy does not equally enjoin it - It will be worthy of a free, enlightened, and at no distant period, a great nation, to give to mankind the magnanimous and too novel example of a people always guided by an exalted justice and benevolence. Who can doubt that, in the course of time and things, the fruits of such a plan would richly repay any temporary advantages which might be lost by a steady adherence to it? Can it be that Providence has not connected the permanent felicity of a nation with its virtue? The experiment, at least, is recommended by every sentiment which ennobles human nature. Alas! is it rendered impossible by its vices?

In the execution of such a plan, nothing is more essential than that permanent, inveterate antipathies against particular nations, and passionate attachments for others, should be excluded; and that, in place of them, just and amicable feelings towards all should be cultivated. The nation which indulges towards another a habitual hatred or a habitual fondness is in some degree a slave. It is a slave to its animosity or to its affection, either of which is sufficient to lead it astray from its duty and its interest. Antipathy in one nation against another disposes each more readily to offer insult and injury, to lay hold of slight causes of umbrage, and to be haughty and intractable, when accidental or trifling occasions of dispute occur. Hence, frequent collisions, obstinate, envenomed, and bloody contests. The nation, prompted by ill-will and resentment, sometimes impels to war the government, contrary to the best calculations of policy. The government sometimes participates in the national propensity, and adopts through passion what reason would reject; at other times it makes the animosity of the nation subservient to projects of hostility instigated by pride, ambition, and other sinister and pernicious motives. The peace often, sometimes perhaps the liberty, of nations, has been the victim.

So likewise, a passionate attachment of one nation for another produces a variety of evils. Sympathy for the favorite nation, facilitating the illusion of an imaginary common interest in cases where no real common interest exists, and infusing into one the enmities of the other, betrays the former into a participation in the quarrels and wars of the latter without adequate inducement or justification. It leads also to concessions to the favorite nation of privileges denied to others which is apt doubly to injure the nation making the concessions; by unnecessarily parting with what ought to have been retained, and by exciting jealousy, ill-will, and a disposition to retaliate, in the parties from whom equal privileges are withheld. And it gives to ambitious, corrupted, or deluded citizens (who devote themselves to the favorite nation), facility to betray or sacrifice the interests of their own country, without odium, sometimes even with popularity; gilding, with the appearances of a virtuous sense of obligation, a commendable deference for public opinion, or a laudable zeal for public good, the base or foolish compliances of ambition, corruption, or infatuation.

As avenues to foreign influence in innumerable ways, such attachments are particularly alarming to the truly enlightened and independent patriot. How many opportunities do they afford to tamper with domestic factions, to practice the arts of seduction, to mislead public opinion, to influence or awe the public councils. Such an attachment of a small or weak towards a great and powerful nation dooms the former to be the satellite of the latter.

Against the insidious wiles of foreign influence (I conjure you to believe me, fellow-citizens) the jealousy of a free people ought to be constantly awake, since history and experience prove that foreign influence is one of the most baneful foes of republican government. But that jealousy to be useful must be impartial; else it becomes the instrument of the very influence to be avoided, instead of a defense against it. Excessive partiality for one foreign nation and excessive dislike of another cause those whom they actuate to see danger only on one side, and serve to veil and even second the arts of influence on the other. Real patriots who may resist the intrigues of the favorite are liable to become suspected and odious, while its tools and dupes usurp the applause and confidence of the people, to surrender their interests.

The great rule of conduct for us in regard to foreign nations is in extending our commercial relations, to have with them as little political connection as possible. So far as we have already formed engagements, let them be fulfilled with perfect good faith. Here let us stop. Europe has a set of primary interests which to us have none; or a very remote relation. Hence she must be engaged in frequent controversies, the causes of which are essentially foreign to our concerns. Hence, therefore, it must be unwise in us to implicate ourselves by artificial ties in the ordinary vicissitudes of her politics, or the ordinary combinations and collisions of her friendships or enmities.

Our detached and distant situation invites and enables us to pursue a different course. If we remain one people under an efficient government. the period is not far off when we may defy material injury from external annoyance; when we may take such an attitude as will cause the neutrality we may at any time resolve upon to be scrupulously respected; when belligerent nations, under the impossibility of making acquisitions upon us, will not lightly hazard the giving us provocation; when we may choose peace or war, as our interest, guided by justice, shall counsel.

Why forego the advantages of so peculiar a situation? Why quit our own to stand upon foreign ground? Why, by interweaving our destiny with that of any part of Europe, entangle our peace and prosperity in the toils of European ambition, rivalship, interest, humor or caprice?

It is our true policy to steer clear of permanent alliances with any portion of the foreign world; so far, I mean, as we are now at liberty to do it; for let me not be understood as capable of patronizing infidelity to existing engagements. I hold the maxim no less applicable to public than to private affairs, that honesty is always the best policy. I repeat it, therefore, let those engagements be observed in their genuine sense. But, in my opinion, it is unnecessary and would be unwise to extend them.

Taking care always to keep ourselves by suitable establishments on a respectable defensive posture, we may safely trust to temporary alliances for extraordinary emergencies.

Harmony, liberal intercourse with all nations, are recommended by policy, humanity, and interest. But even our commercial policy should hold an equal and impartial hand; neither seeking nor granting exclusive favors or preferences; consulting the natural course of things; diffusing and diversifying by gentle means the streams of commerce, but forcing nothing; establishing (with powers so disposed, in order to give trade a stable course, to define the rights of our merchants, and to enable the government to support them) conventional rules of intercourse, the best that present circumstances and mutual opinion will permit, but temporary, and liable to be from time to time abandoned or varied, as experience and circumstances shall dictate; constantly keeping in view that it is folly in one nation to look for disinterested favors from another; that it must pay with a portion of its independence for whatever it may accept under that character; that, by such acceptance, it may place itself in the condition of having given equivalents for nominal favors, and yet of being reproached with ingratitude for not giving more. There can be no greater error than to expect or calculate upon real favors from nation to nation. It is an illusion, which experience must cure, which a just pride ought to discard.

In offering to you, my countrymen, these counsels of an old and affectionate friend, I dare not hope they will make the strong and lasting impression I could wish; that they will control the usual current of the passions, or prevent our nation from running the course which has hitherto marked the destiny of nations. But, if I may even flatter myself that they may be productive of some partial benefit, some occasional good; that they may now and then recur to moderate the fury of party spirit, to warn against the mischiefs of foreign intrigue, to guard against the impostures of pretended patriotism; this hope will be a full recompense for the solicitude for your welfare, by which they have been dictated.

How far in the discharge of my official duties I have been guided by the principles which have been delineated, the public records and other evidences of my conduct must witness to you and to the world. To myself, the assurance of my own conscience is, that I have at least believed myself to be guided by them.

In relation to the still subsisting war in Europe, my proclamation of the twenty-second of April, 1793, is the index of my plan. Sanctioned by your approving voice, and by that of your representatives in both houses of Congress, the spirit of that measure has continually governed me, uninfluenced by any attempts to deter or divert me from it.

After deliberate examination, with the aid of the best lights I could obtain, I was well satisfied that our country, under all the circumstances of the case, had a right to take, and was bound in duty and interest to take, a neutral position. Having taken it, I determined, as far as should depend upon me, to maintain it, with moderation, perseverance, and firmness.

The considerations which respect the right to hold this conduct, it is not necessary on this occasion to detail. I will only observe that, according to my understanding of the matter, that right, so far from being denied by any of the belligerent powers, has been virtually admitted by all.

The duty of holding a neutral conduct may be inferred, without anything more, from the obligation which justice and humanity impose on every nation, in cases in which it is free to act, to maintain inviolate the relations of peace and amity towards other nations.

The inducements of interest for observing that conduct will best be referred to your own reflections and experience. With me a predominant motive has been to endeavor to gain time to our country to settle and mature its yet recent institutions, and to progress without interruption to that degree of strength and consistency which is necessary to give it, humanly speaking, the command of its own fortunes.

Though, in reviewing the incidents of my administration, I am unconscious of intentional error, I am nevertheless too sensible of my defects not to think it probable that I may have committed many errors. Whatever they may be, I fervently beseech the Almighty to avert or mitigate the evils to which they may tend. I shall also carry with me the hope that my country will never cease to view them with indulgence; and that, after forty five years of my life dedicated to its service with an upright zeal, the faults of incompetent abilities will be consigned to oblivion, as myself must soon be to the mansions of rest.

Relying on its kindness in this as in other things, and actuated by that fervent love towards it, which is so natural to a man who views in it the native soil of himself and his progenitors for several generations, I anticipate with pleasing expectation that retreat in which I promise myself to realize, without alloy, the sweet enjoyment of partaking, in the midst of my fellow-citizens, the benign influence of good laws under a free government, the ever-favorite object of my heart, and the happy reward, as I trust, of our mutual cares, labors, and dangers.

Notes

Introduction
1. America's God and Country encyclopedia of quotations by William J. Federer

Chapter 1
1-5 America's God and Country encyclopedia of quotations by William J. Federer

Presidential images

https://en.wikipedia.org/wiki/George_Washington

https://en.wikipedia.org/wiki/John_Adams

6. https://stream.org/the-founders-on-immigration/

7. George Washington farewell address

Chapter 2

1-9 *America's God and Country encyclopedia of quotations* by William J. Federer

10. Adoniram Judson- https://en.wikipedia.org/wiki/Adoniram_Judson

Chapter 3

1-7 http://ppfc.org/quotes.htm

8. https://en.wikipedia.org/wiki/Brown_Bess

9. https://en.wikipedia.org/wiki/M249_light_machine_gun

10. https://www.monticello.org/site/research-and-collections/tyranny-defined-which-legal-government-spurious-quotation

11. Quotation from the Constitution of the United States of America

Chapter 4

1. https://www.azquotes.com/author/7392-Thomas_Jefferson/tag/integrity

2. *America's God and Country encyclopedia of quotations* by William J. Federer

Chapter 5

1. George Washington farewell address

Chapter 6

1. https://www.goodreads.com/quotes/333268-if-we-lose-freedom-here-there-is-no-place-to

2. https://www.wnd.com/2009/01/85442/

3. https://ivarfjeld.com/2011/01/25/obama-all-nations-must-build-global-regime/

4. https://www.climatedepot.com/2012/11/21/flashback-gore-us-climate-bill-will-help-bring-about-global-governance/

5. http://edition.cnn.com/2009/WORLD/europe/02/22/germany.financial.summit/index.html

6. https://www.goodreads.com/quotes/162688-since-i-entered-politics-i-have-chiefly-had-men-s-views

7. https://www.youtube.com/watch?v=QeYgLLahHv8

8. http://www.arewelivinginthelastdays.com/com/quotes.html

9. http://en.wikipedia.org/wiki/Georgia_Guidestones

10. http://en.wikipedia.org/wiki/Jack_Kilby

11. http://article.wn.com/view/2010/08/29/Japans_smart_toilet_can_keep_your_health_in_check/

12. http://www.memorymedallion.com/

13. Verichip http://en.wikipedia.org/wiki/

14. *America's God and Country encyclopedia of quotations*

by William J. Federer

The Constitution of The United States constitutioncenter.org/media/files/constitution.pdf

The Declaration of Independence archives.gov/founding-docs/declaration-transcript

"Give Me Liberty Or Give Me Death!" Speech by Patrick Henry colonialwilliamsburg.org/learn/deep-dives/give-me-liberty-or-give-me-death/

Boston Massacre Oration by Joseph Warren drjosephwarren.com/2015/03/warren's-1775-boston-massacre-oration-in-full-text-our-country-is-in-danger-but-not-to-be-despaired-of/

Patrick Henry Speech to the Virginia Convention archive.csac.history.wisc.edu/Patrick_Henry_Speech_in_the_virginia_Convention(2).pdf
First Inaugural Address George Washington archives.gov/exhibits/american_originals/inaugtxt.html

AN AMERICAN HISTORY: OUR FOUNDATION AND MORAL COMPASS

Farewell Address George Washington
ourdocuments.gov/doc.php?flash=false&doc=15&page=transcript

WOODROW POLSTON

About the Author

Woodrow Polston is the Author of numerous books that are attributed to biblical studies. The President of Polston house Publishing, Woodrow is a licensed Minister and political activist who resides in rural Missouri. *To learn more, visit Polstonhouse.com!*

WOODROW POLSTON

AN AMERICAN HISTORY: OUR FOUNDATION AND MORAL COMPASS

Available from Polstonhouse.com

AN AMERICAN HISTORY: OUR FOUNDATION AND MORAL COMPASS

Available from Polstonhouse.com

AN AMERICAN HISTORY: OUR FOUNDATION AND MORAL COMPASS

Available from Polstonhouse.com

Pocket size! (4 x 6)

WOODROW POLSTON

Available from Polstonhouse.com

AN AMERICAN HISTORY: OUR FOUNDATION AND MORAL COMPASS

Available from Polstonhouse.com

AN AMERICAN HISTORY: OUR FOUNDATION AND MORAL COMPASS

Available from Polstonhouse.com

AN AMERICAN HISTORY: OUR FOUNDATION AND MORAL COMPASS

WOODROW POLSTON

www.ingramcontent.com/pod-product-compliance
Lightning Source LLC
Chambersburg PA
CBHW060521100426
42743CB00009B/1397